JACK FITZGERALD'S
Notebook

Revised Edition

Jack Fitzgerald

Other Jack Fitzgerald books from Creative Book Publishing

Amazing Newfoundland Stories	ISBN 0-920021-36-0	$9.95
Strange But True Newfoundland Stories	ISBN 0-920021-57-3	$9.95
Newfoundland Fireside Stories	ISBN 0-920021-78-6	$9.95
Where Angels Fear To Tread	ISBN 0-895387-49-3	$11.95
Another Time, Another Place	ISBN 1-895387-75-2	$11.95
The Hangman is Never Late	ISBN 1-894294-02-5	$12.95
Beyond Belief	ISBN 1-894294-31-9	$12.95

Ask your favourite bookstore or order directly from the publisher.

Creative Book Publishing
P.O. Box 8660
36 Austin Street
St. John's, NF
A1B 3T7

phone: (709) 722-8500
fax: (709) 579-7745
e-mail: books@rb.nf.ca

Please add $5.00 Canadian for shipping and handling and taxes on single book orders and $1.00 for each additional book.

JACK FITZGERALD'S Notebook

Revised Edition

Jack Fitzgerald

St. John's, Newfoundland
2002

©2002 Jack Fitzgerald

Le Conseil des Arts | The Canada Council
du Canada | for the Arts

We acknowledge the support of The Canada Council for the Arts for our
publishing program.

We acknowledge the financial support of the Government of Canada through the Book
Publishing Industry Development Program (BPIDP) for our publishing program.

Cover Art and Design: Maurice Fitzgerald

∞ Printed on acid-free paper

Published by
CREATIVE BOOK PUBLISHING
a division of 10366 Newfoundland Limited
a Robinson-Blackmore Printing & Publishing associated company
P.O. Box 8660, St. John's, Newfoundland A1B 3T7

A revised edition of *Jack Fitzgerald's Notebook*
originally published in 1985 under ISBN 0-920021-25-5, five printings

Printed in Canada by:
ROBINSON-BLACKMORE PRINTING & PUBLISHING

National Library of Canada Cataloguing in Publication Data

Fitzgerald, Jack, 1945-
    Jack Fitzgerald's notebook

Rev. ed.
ISBN 1-894294-40-8

    1. Newfoundland–History–Anecdotes. 2. Newfoundland–
Biography--Anecdotes. I. Title.

FC2161.8.F58 2001   971.8   C2001-904157-8
F1122.6.F582 2001

Dedicated to
the memory of
Frank and Rose Jackman

CONTENTS

GHOSTS, THE SUPERNATURAL AND OTHER MYSTERIES

CRIME AND JUSTICE

WAR, BATTLES AND MILITARY HEROES

TRAGEDIES, NATURAL DISASTERS AND HUMAN ERROR

Politics and Religion

Rare and Remarkable Newfoundlanders

Miscellaneous Stories

INTRODUCTION

Jack Fitzgerald's Notebook is a collection of unusual, amazing and offbeat stories from Newfoundland's past. These stories of pirates, treasures, murder, ghosts, Newfoundlanders who distinguished themselves in other parts of the world, heroes, and adventure stories were gathered from numerous records preserved at the Provincial Archives and the Newfoundland Historical Society. Other stories were gathered from storytellers and some come from Newfoundland folklore.

While most of the material is historically correct and easily verified, other parts, especially those stories handed down from generation to generation, are not as easily confirmed. Nevertheless, all stories are a valuable part of our Newfoundland legends, folklore and history and I hope the reader will find them as interesting and entertaining as I did in collecting them.

The late Dr. Robbie Robertson deserves special thanks for her endless patience and co-operation in helping me track down material for the book and for her outstanding work at the Newfoundland Historical Society in maintaining up-to-date and exhaustive filing records.

NOTORIOUS PIRATES, BURIED TREASURE AND SEA ADVENTURES

The Irish Princess Who Married a Newfoundlander

Sir Hugh O'Connor of County Connacht, Ireland, was the claimant to the Irish throne. The ongoing struggle between Irish and English patriots was causing a rift among the inhabitants of Sir Hugh's county. The struggle resulted in a split in the Irish royal family which caused Sir Hugh to become concerned for the safety of his daughter, Princess Sheila. Sir Hugh made arrangements for the princess to be sent to a convent in France where her aunt was the abbess.

While en route to France, Dutch pirates captured the Irish ship, looted it and took Princess Sheila captive. However, before the pirates could get their prize to port they were intercepted and captured by Captain Peter Easton, who later became one of Newfoundland's most infamous pirates. At that time Easton was the commander of a fleet of British warships. Princess Sheila was taken on board Easton's ship which was heading for Newfoundland. Easton was being sent to this island by the British king to protect the English fishing fleet.

During the trip the princess met and fell in love with Easton's lieutenant, Gilbert Pike. Captain Easton arranged for his ship's chaplain to marry the two. Upon arriving at Harbour Grace, Pike and his Irish princess decided to settle down at Mosquito, a community now known as Bristol Hope. They had two children and the Pikes played a major part in developing that community. Princess Sheila, who had managed to conceal her identity as an Irish princess, was recognized by Irish immigrants who added the Gaelic name Nageira to her title. Nageira is the Gaelic word for beauty and Princess Sheila was described by many as a natural leader and a most beautiful lady. Then one day tragedy struck Bristol Hope. The community was attacked by pirates. Princess Sheila gathered the women and children and hid them in the nearby hills. Her husband Gilbert Pike was taken by the pirates and never heard from again. Princess Sheila moved with her children to Carbonear where she died on August 4, 1753, at the age of 105. Newfoundland's Irish princess is buried in the garden of Hubert Soper of Carbonear.

The Trouble with Dates

There is some difficulty interpreting 1753 as the burial date for Princess Sheila. Peter Easton was a serving naval officer (or possibly a privateer) prior to 1610 when he became actively involved in piracy, a trade which he followed for about ten years (after which he settled in the south of France and lived to a healthy and prosperous old age). Princess Sheila is believed to have been rescued by him in 1602, and, assuming that she was at least sixteen at the time, a more reasonable burial year would have been 1690 or there about. A certain amount of factual information is available about Peter Easton and Gilbert Pike. Sheila's story, being more anecdotal in nature, is more difficult to document. If she did die in 1753 at the age of 105, she could not have been rescued by Easton (150 years earlier) and then subsequently marry Gilbert Pike.

It is possible that the date on the tombstone is an error. There appears to have been no tracing or rubbing made of the actual words on the tombstone, and since the stone itself has long been worn smooth, it is not possible at this time to authenticate the early documentation. It is also possible that Princess Sheila was not rescued by Peter Easton but by some other privateer (of which there were many) at a later time and with the telling and re-telling of the story, the facts have been adjusted to fit the legend. It is difficult to prove the legend one way or another, but it does make a wonderful and romantic story. And the Pike family is prominent in Carbonear to this day. (ed.)

PETER EASTON

When the world renowned Newfoundland pirate Peter Easton voluntarily retired from piracy to settle at Villefranche, Savoy, he took with him almost $7 million in gold. At Villefranche, Easton purchased a palace and developed a close friendship with the Duke of Savoy whose own wealth was only a fraction of Easton's. Easton was given respectability by being granted the title Marquis of Savoy. The wealthy Marquis was only forty years old at the time of his retirement from piracy. He added to his wealth by marrying a very rich French lady.

While a pirate in Newfoundland, Easton kidnaped Sir Richard Whitbourne, governor of Newfoundland, and held him prisoner on Kelly's Island for eleven weeks. Easton tried to persuade the able Whitbourne to join him as his chief lieutenant. When he saw the uselessness of his efforts, he managed to persuade Whitbourne to go to England and seek for him a royal pardon.

When Whitbourne arrived in London he learned

that a pardon had already been granted. That pardon never reached Easton. A second pardon was issued on November 26, 1612, with Captain Roger Middleton being commissioned to deliver it. By the time Middleton got to Newfoundland, Easton had despaired of ever getting a pardon and had left. By that time Easton had five hundred men and a large fleet of ships. Unlike the loyalist Mainwaring who never attacked an English ship, Easton attacked any and all nationalities. He left Newfoundland and for a short time joined with other pirates on the Barbary Coast.

Easton amassed his wealth over a relatively short period of time. He came to Newfoundland in 1611 with ten ships. Over the following ten year period, his company of pirates grew from one hundred to five hundred. He captured millions in property and treasure, some of it perhaps still buried here in Newfoundland.

A BIG SCANDAL WITH A NEWFOUNDLAND CONNECTION

The Cobham family of France were wealthy, powerful and influential. They had their own private harbour, a yacht which was the envy of many of their aristocratic friends, and a palatial mansion. They also had a closely guarded secret — a secret shared only by the senior Cobhams, Eric and Maria. Maria eventually took an overdose of poison and jumped from a cliff, while Eric, tormented by remorse, summoned a Roman Catholic priest to his death bed, confessed his secret and begged for absolution. He then handed the priest a lengthy written document containing the Cobham's terrible secret which he made the priest promise to have published after he passed on.

Days later Eric passed away and the priest arranged for the publication of the Cobham confession. When the Cobham heirs learned of the newly released book they travelled all over France buying up copies. Fortunately they didn't get all the books, and at least one is preserved in the archives at Paris. The book tells a long tale of piracy, murder and sadistic torture, much of which took place in Newfoundland.

At the age of twenty-one Cobham started his sinful career by smuggling ten thousand gallons of brandy into England from France, a deed that got him two years at Newgate prison. He later stole a fortune from a hotel guest. The hotel owner was arrested and hung for that offence. Cobham meanwhile used the stolen money to launch a pirate's career. He purchased a ship, mounted it with fourteen guns and recruited a crew from London taverns. Before leaving England he met and married Maria Lindsay, an adventurous, sadistically demented female who relished her new life as a murdering pirate. On one occasion she ran her cutlass through the heart of a ship's captain and took his uniform. When the ship's officers complained, she had them tied to the capstan and riddled with bullets. On another occasion she disposed of captured seamen near Corner Brook by sewing them into bags and tossing them into the sea. Once she took the crew of a West Indies ship and calmed them down by offering them a home cooked meal of stew. The relaxed sailors ate to their heart's content, not knowing Maria had laced the stew with laudanum, her favourite poison.

After twenty years of piracy and after amassing a great fortune the Cobhams left Corner Brook to retire in France. French authorities impressed by the Cobham's wealth had Eric Cobham appointed a French magistrate. As the years passed, the yearning for piracy surfaced occasionally and Maria would put on her pirate suit and with her husband the magistrate, would sail out into the Atlantic in search of Spanish ships to plunder.

THE GENTLEMAN PIRATE

Henry Mainwaring was a graduate of Oxford who held a law degree and is considered by historians to be the founder of the great British navy. Yet at the age of twenty-four he led a band of four hundred Newfoundland pirates in a short outlaw career which so angered the King of Spain that he sent a small fleet of the Spanish navy to put an end to Mainwaring's plundering of Spanish possessions.

While still a lawyer and friend of King James I, he was asked by the king to lead an expedition to Newfoundland to stop the notorious pirate Peter Easton who had been using Newfoundland as a base for his operations. By the time Mainwaring arrived in Newfoundland waters, he had come to the conclusion that he had a better chance of accumulating wealth as a pirate than as a lawyer, so he raised the Jolly Roger and enlisted four hundred men from ports around Newfoundland for his fleet then sailed off to the Barbary Coast.

But even as a pirate, Mainwaring remained an English gentleman and loyal to the British Crown. Whenever he captured a Spanish ship with goods heading to an English port he made sure the goods were delivered. He never attacked a British vessel. On one occasion Spanish pirates had captured the whole Newfoundland fishing fleet and Mainwaring came to the rescue. He freed the fleet and took £500,000 in gold coins from the pirates which were destined for King Philip of Spain.

The Spanish king was so outraged by Mainwaring and his army of Newfoundlanders that he sent five warships to hunt them down and teach them a lesson. Six weeks later the Spanish warships sailed back into Madrid harbour badly beaten. They had caught up with Mainwaring but were taught a few lessons themselves. King Philip then offered Mainwaring a pardon, the position of commander of the Spanish navy and twenty thousand gold ducats a year to join him and give up piracy. When Mainwaring refused, Philip requested the help of his friend the King of England. King James offered Mainwaring a pardon which he accepted. Henry Mainwaring became Sir Henry Mainwaring and was made vice admiral of the British navy. During the British civil war he backed the losing side and was sent into exile at Jersey with King Charles.

Mainwaring also wrote two books, one on seamanship and the second entitled, *Of the Beginnings, Practices and Suppression of Pirates*, a subject he knew well. Eventually Sir Henry returned from exile in Jersey and died a near pauper in England in 1653.

An Unlikely Pirate

When Captain John Mason was released from a Scottish prison after serving time for piracy, King

James I appointed him as the second governor of Newfoundland. This seemed a strange sort of thing to do, yet John Mason was not an ordinary pirate. He had earned the friendship and loyalty of the king when he was only twenty years old. At that time he led an expedition of four ships and successfully reclaimed the Hebrides for the king from a pirate organization known as the Red Shanks.

Mason's thirst for adventure continued throughout his tenure as governor and he explored Newfoundland producing the first known English map of the island. That same map was reproduced in William Vaughan's famous book, *The Golden Fleece*. Mason tried to attract new settlers to this country by writing an article entitled, "A Brief Discourse on Newfoundland," which described our geography, climate and natural resources.

When England went to war with Spain during the mid seventeenth century the king appointed Mason to the position of treasurer and paymaster of the British forces. When the war ended the king once more bestowed favours upon his pirate friend. This time he gave him a grant of land in America which later became the states of New Hampshire and Maine. There were other honours for Captain John Mason. King James appointed him commissioner of all forts and castles in England; judge of the courts in Hampshire; vice-admiral of New England and commander of the South Sea Castle, the most important fortress in England located at the entry to Portsmouth harbour.

It was Mason's wife Anne who taught the famous American Indian Squantum to speak English and converted him to the Church of England faith. Along with being the second governor of Newfoundland, Mason is credited in American history as being founder of the state of New Hampshire. After his death Captain Mason was buried at Westminster Abbey. Not bad for a rehabilitated pirate!

FAMOUS ENGLISH PIRATE ATTACKS NEWFOUNDLAND PORTS

One of the many notorious pirates to plunder ports in Newfoundland was the English pirate Edward Lowe. Lowe was born at Westminster, England, around the turn of the eighteenth century and began his career as a thief on the streets near the historic House of Commons.

When Lowe was about sixteen he went to sea with another brother and for a long period he sailed the seven seas and built a reputation for himself through-out the world, a pirate's reputation.

His career as a pirate had its beginning in Honduras Bay when he and twelve shipmates mutinied. They took control of their ship and launched their plundering careers. From that point Lowe's life became a long list of cruelties and terror which were heightened a little later when he sailed to the Grand Cayman and joined forces with another notorious scoundrel, George Lowther.

During the summer of 1722, Lowe and his crew set sail for Newfoundland. They left Port Roseway and after several weeks at sea arrived off The Narrows of St. John's. It was a foggy day as they prepared to enter the narrow St. John's harbour where they intended to murder and plunder. When the fog lifted, they saw a ship which looked prosperous to them and decided to make it their first target.

Lowe ordered all except six men below deck so the vessel would pass as a fishing schooner. The ship was called the *Fancy* and as she moved past the narrows, a small fishing boat pulled alongside. The pirates were planning to take the wealthy looking ship by surprise. Lowe shouted to the fishermen on the small vessel near them and asked if they were going out fishing. The crew answered that they were and asked Lowe what shipping port he came from.

The pirate answered, "From Barbados with a cargo of rum and sugar." Then Lowe asked the fishermen the name of the prosperous looking ship in the harbour. The pirate chief nearly fainted when he was told it was the HMS *Solebay*, a powerful man-of-war.

Lowe wasted no time in getting as far away from St. John's as he could possibly get. They moved into the port of Carbonear where they plundered and robbed. They took seven vessels from Carbonear fishermen and headed for the Grand Banks.

Lowe continued his attacks on Newfoundland ports until he was chased out of the country by the 44th Regiment . . . once and for all.

JEAN ANGO

The name Jean Ango is not as well known in the history of Newfoundland piracy as are those of Captain Peter Easton, Henry Mainwaring, John Mason or Captain Kelly. However, Ango of Dieppe, was the first known pirate to operate from Newfoundland waters. Ango was a prominent French merchant adventurer who sailed the oceans for King Francis I just as Sir Francis Drake had sailed for Queen Elizabeth I. When

Ango plundered Newfoundland in 1520, King Francis was the most powerful monarch in all Europe, and he and Ango agreed to split any loot recovered in Ango's piracy career.

Prior to piracy, Ango served his country well in Newfoundland. Using French naval convoys under his command, he established the French fisheries in Newfoundland on a solid basis. When he first arrived here in 1520, he led a great squadron of armed ships. His two chief lieutenants were known as the notorious Parmentier brothers.

Once Ango turned to piracy, no ship was safe. Ango captured and sacked all the French fishing vessels and premises in eastern Newfoundland. After plundering this area he sailed off to Brazil, up through the Antilles and back to Newfoundland before returning to France to give the king his share of the booty. Ango kept up his raids in Newfoundland for twenty years and like the pirates that followed him in later years, he took his fortune and settled in Europe.

While in Europe, the Portuguese, with good reason, captured and burnt some of his ships. Ango sent a note to the king of Portugal demanding reparation for his loss. The Portuguese ignored the demand and Ango called together his squadron and attacked Lisbon. In order to lift the siege, the king of Portugal came to terms with Ango and gave him back what his men had stolen.

Ango built a large castle in Normandy, styled after an ancient court, with a huge manor house and a rectangular court enclosed by a farm building. The castle is well preserved to this day and is a tourist attraction. In spite of his great wealth Ango found himself the victim of a number of lawsuits from prominent French creditors. He died in poverty in 1551.

The Pirates' Secret Contract

Captain Bart Roberts (a.k.a. Black Bart) was as blood thirsty as any pirate but he had a strict code of ethics which he expected his men to follow. Roberts captured or sank four hundred ships in one year, establishing a record among pirates which held for one hundred years. On one of his plundering escapades around Newfoundland's coast he took a group of Newfoundlanders aboard as crew members. Before becoming a full-fledged pirate, however, each one had to sign the pirates' contract and swear on Bart's personal bible to abide by its conditions.

Recently I came across one of Bart's contracts which provides an interesting insight into one's life as a pirate. The contract reads as follows:

1. Every man has a vote in the affairs of the movement and equal title to provisions and liquors.
2. Every man to be called fairly in turn to serve on board of prizes (pirates term for captured ships) and on those occasions allowed a shift of clothing. If a pirate defrauded the company of a dollar in jewels or money, marooning was the punishment. This meant being deserted on a island with just a gun and a bottle of water. If they robbed from each other the guilty one got his nose or ear slit.
3. No person allowed to play cards or dice for money.

4. Lights and candles must be out by eight o'clock each night. Any drinking after eight o'clock was permitted only on the bottom deck.
5. Each man must keep his gun, pistol and cutlass clean and ready for service.
6. No boy or woman to be among them.
7. To desert their ship in battle was punished by death or marooning.
8. No striking any man on board, but every man's quarrel to be ended ashore and the bosun to act as umpire.
9. No man to break up his way of living until each had shared one thousand pounds. If any man lost a limb or became crippled in service, he was given eight hundred dollars from the common stock.
10. The musicians to have rest on the Sabbath but the other six days and nights without special favours.
11. If a man strikes another he shall receive Moses Law. (Forty lashes on the bare back less one).
12. If a man smoked tobacco in the hold without a cap to his pipe or carried an uncovered candle he got the same.
13. If a man meddled with a prudent woman without her consent he would be executed.

Three Newfoundlanders who tried to desert Bart's

ship at Barbados were captured and given a pirates' trial with Roberts presiding. One of the pirates took a liking to Harry Gadsby from the southwest coast of Newfoundland and defended him, using the strongest and foulest of the pirate language. He got Gadsby off with a strong warning while the other two Newfoundlanders were tied to the masthead and shot. Captain Bart Roberts was later killed during a bloody battle with the British vessel the *Swallow*. His body was thrown into the sea.

PIRATES GOLD

During the seventeenth and eighteenth centuries Newfoundland was a haven for pirates. Pirates like the famous Peter Easton, Captain John Mason, Bart Roberts and Sir Henry Mainwaring, all used this province at one time as a base for their operations. It is not surprising then that over the years buried treasure and pirates' gold have been found in many parts of the island.

A fortune in gold was recovered from a small island near Baccalieu just thirty-eight miles out from Kelly's Island, a former headquarters for Peter Easton. Four fishermen from Grate's Cove, while fishing in the area, found an unusual looking large wine bottle lying in sea water near the shore. The fishermen at first thought they had found a bottle of sand because it weighed so much. However when they broke it open, Spanish gold ducats fell everywhere. The men agreed to share their findings equally and to remain silent about it. Three of them moved to the United States with their shares while the captain remained at Grate's Cove keeping his commitment to remain silent.

Just before his death he revealed the secret to his family and passed over a small bag of gold to his son. The story got out and people from all over the bay began searching for Spanish gold. One man from Trinity found a square box containing a huge fortune of gold and silver.

Another discovery of pirate treasure took place during the 1950s again in an area once habited by Peter Easton and his company of five hundred pirates. Two men from New York hired a fisherman at Kelligrews to take them on a camping trip to Kelly's Island.

After almost a week on the island the two packed their gear and arranged for the fisherman to return them from Kelly's Island. Shortly after, they left the province. When the fisherman hauled up his boat to drain it for the winter he discovered several gold coins, all from the reign of Elizabeth I. Since then, there have been many treasure hunting expeditions to Kelly's Island.

JOHN KEATING'S SECRET

When Simon Bolivar led his forces from the hillsides of Peru towards its capital at Lima, authorities in that city were in a panic to smuggle seventy million dollars in gold and jewels out of the country. They found a temporary hiding place in the Cathedral of Lima, but as Bolivar neared the city they rushed the treasure to the waterfront hoping to get it out of the country. In desperation they entrusted the great fortune to a Newfoundland sea captain named William Thompson of the brig *Mary Dear*. But they picked the wrong man! Thompson sailed out of Lima and the Peruvians never saw their treasure again. They did trail Thompson throughout the Caribbean and managed to capture and hang some of his crew members.

Meanwhile, Thompson buried the treasure on Cocos Island and returned to hide out in Newfoundland. While in St. John's he befriended a ship's carpenter named John Keating and told him of the treasure. Governor LeMarchant learned the whereabouts of Thompson, who was wanted by British authorities for piracy, and once again Thompson was on the run. However, this time there was no place to go. He was found in a bank of snow at Bay Bulls, having died of exposure. Yet legend has it that Thompson was the victim of a Peruvian Indian curse.

Thompson's death left the field open for Keating who solicited the help of a Captain Boag and set out to find the Cocos treasure. Although they were successful in locating the treasure, the crew mutinied at the sight of such enormous wealth. Captain Boag filled his pockets with gold and jumped into a dory which capsized, drowning him as he was weighted down by the gold. Keating however, made it back to St. John's and took with him thousands of dollars in gold.

Keating never returned to seek the remainder of the treasure but before he passed away he told of its location to two people. During the 1840s he became shipwrecked in the St. Lawrence River area and was rescued by Captain Nick Fitzgerald of Harbour Grace. In gratitude for the rescue Keating told Fitzgerald of the treasure. Shortly after returning to St. John's he became ill and died. Before his death he told his daughter, Mrs. Richard Young, of the treasure's location.

Captain Fitzgerald formed a company with retired British Admiral Hugh Palliser to search for the gold while Keating's daughter teamed up with German explorer Van Brewer to seek it. Word of the Cocos treasure spread and so many attempts were made to find it that the Costa Rican government implemented a $1,000 per month treasure hunting fee at Cocos.

THE PIRATES OF TREASURE COVE

If you knew Captain Jack Dodd of Torbay, you would never forget him. I knew Captain Jack well and spent many hours at his Bauline Line home listening to his fascinating repertoire of Newfoundland stories. Dodd realized one of his life long dreams when *Wind in the Rigging*, an autobiography of the Captain was published. In 1976, a few years after its publication, Captain Jack Dodd died at his new home in Harbour Grace.

One of the fascinating stories I recall hearing the Old Captain tell as we sipped tea around his homemade wooden kitchen table, was the story of the pirates of Treasure Cove, a cove better known today as Tapper's Cove. In that ominous seaman type tone of conversation that only Jack Dodd could deliver, he told of how the older residents of Torbay avoided Tapper's Cove at night because of the frequent apparitions of a headless young boy and a phantom Newfoundland dog.

According to Dodd the story had its beginning in the seventeenth century when pirates captured a Spanish galleon loaded with gold for the Spanish treasury and brought it to Tapper's Cove to loot. Most of the gold was taken off when another pirate ship flying the Jolly Roger sailed into Torbay and battled the pirates for possession of the galleon.

Having driven its original captors into the hills of Torbay, the attacking pirates removed the rest of the gold and scuttled the galleon off the shore at Tapper's Cove.

The legend of the Tapper's Cove treasure was first told to Captain Jack around 1920 by a Mrs. Gosse at Torbay who was almost ninety years old at the time. Dodd said according to the story handed down, the pirates dug an artificial stream through rock at the top of Treasure Cove. They made a wooden bottom for the stream which somehow was connected to the place where the treasure was hidden. Before leaving Newfoundland they selected a young boy and his dog to guard the treasure. The superstitious pirates cut off the boy's head and killed the dog in the belief their spirits would protect the buried treasure.

Well, it was another colourful Newfoundland story but there seemed to be little basis in fact. That was until a year later when Captain Jack, fishing off Chair Cove, found his net entangled. When he managed to drag it on board his dory he discovered a piece of fancy carved oak from the keel of a ship. Recalling the pirate story Jack spent the following weeks scouring the Tapper Cove area. He found a Spanish gold coin with the inscription *1784, Carolus, 11, Dei, Gratia, Hispas et Ind. Rex.*

He also found the old pirate well at the cliff on top of Tapper's Cove. There was a wooden bottom in the stream and the wood seemed to be foreign to this country.

Although Jack continued his treasure hunt for years after, he found nothing more, only the encouragement to continue the legend of the pirates of Treasure Cove.

PIRATES, TREASURES AND GHOSTS

Newfoundland folklore is rich with stories of pirate treasures and ghosts. Perhaps the most intriguing of all legends combining both these aspects is the story of the Chapel Cove pirate treasures. Chapel Cove, located in the district of Harbour Main, has long been forgotten as the place where eighteenth century pirates seeking refuge in Newfoundland hid fortunes in buried treasure. In consequence, many attempts were made to locate these treasures with some of them providing the basis for many Chapel Cove stories.

In 1895, Joe Holden, Pat Brich and Peter Gorman set out for Chapel Cove with various digging implements. They began digging at the site they believed contained a large pirate treasure. After labouring for hours they came upon a rust-covered metal chest. No sooner did they strike the chest than a phantom-like vessel, with all sails set, appeared, crossed the cove and steered a direct course for them. The men dropped their tools and ran for safety. Legend has it that they were so frightened by the apparition that they were confined to bed for several days.

Fourteen years passed before another effort was made to find treasure at Chapel Cove. This time the attempt was made by Tom Campbell of Harbour Main. When Campbell struck the chest with a crow bar, a loud noise filled the area causing him to tremble. Then a phantom figure emerged from the open pit and seizing the crowbar, broke it in two.

The next attempt to locate the treasure was more technical and scientific than the others. A train conductor named Spence hired a mineralogist to assist him in his hunt for the treasure. Word of the adventure spread quickly throughout Harbour Main and at one point, Spence had an audience of almost four hundred people.

His Worship J. P. O'Donnell visited the area and was so concerned over the possibility that the crowd would attack Spence if gold was found, that he dispatched a number of local and special constables to control the crowd.

When Spence located a large metal chest, police were assigned to guard it. During the night, three phantom figures appeared, moaning and groaning and causing the startled policemen to drop their bayonets and run. When they returned the next day, the treasure had vanished. It is believed that three local lads had disguised themselves as ghosts and removed the treasure of about $300,000 in gold. Spence was not deterred by this loss. He engaged the services of another mineralogist, Dr. Chandlier, to help him continue the search. They succeeded in finding a small chest filled with gold coins. While looking for other treasures, workmen told of strange noises and phantom-like figures appearing before them. The workers refused to go back to work and Spence discontinued his efforts because he could never again get local workers to assist him.

How Kelly's Island Got Its Name!

Kelly's Island in Conception Bay is named after Captain Kelly, another pirate who at one time operated out of Newfoundland. Kelly, a giant of a man, was leader of a group of slaves on a slave ship sailing past

Newfoundland waters. Kelly broke his chains, freed the slaves, took over the ship and became a blood-thirsty scourge of the seven seas.

Captain Kelly disciplined his men by breaking their backs over his knee. Legend has it that he buried a treasure on Kelly's Island and killed a crew member so the spirit could stand watch over it. At the turn of the century two Conception Bay men set out to find the treasure but their boat was later found empty with a Spanish doubloon in the bottom.

The gold at Chapel Cove, one of the pirate treasures eventually recovered, drew many adventurers before it was discovered. One of these was an old Irishman who set out with a horse drawn cart and an old map. The Irishman, who had heard many tales of pirates' ghosts protecting the Chapel Cove treasure, said that as he approached the head of the port, a ghostly ship suddenly appeared and glided past him on land. When he reached the lake the phantom ship was anchored on the pond. A boat put out and a man in pirate garb came to watch the Irishman dig for gold. The Irishman, claimed he had gone to the area prepared, as he had gotten a church blessing. He was not frightened by the apparitions. When he found the gold the pirate tried to take it from him. During the struggle the Irishman was knocked down. He then bargained with the ghost saying, "If you are a pirate, you can have a pirate's share, a third. I will give it to the church or an orphanage or any charity you like."

The ghost suddenly uttered a loud groan which caused the Irishman to faint. When he came to, he got on his cart and hurried away from the gold. Out of nowhere the phantom ship passed him and sailed out the bay.

Local legend also tells of pirate treasure in and

around St. John's. Near the head of Deadman's Pond on Signal Hill lies a treasure protected by the headless ghost of a giant Negro, left by pirates centuries ago to protect their gold. A pirate's treasure is also hidden near Quidi Vidi and another treasure in a pond close to Shoal Bay.

THOUSANDS HIDDEN ON WATER STREET

Every day hundreds of people walk over concrete steps located in downtown St. John's, completely unaware of the fortune concealed below and the mystery which surrounds its burial.

This story began during the mid-1940s when an employee of a chartered bank embezzled a large sum of money from his employer. The money was stolen over a long period of time and some old-timers say the man used it to purchase a home in the downtown area. The balance of the money was sealed into a metal can and locked. The bank became suspicious and an investigation led to the man's arrest. However before being nabbed by police the man took his metal can and went to a laneway connecting New Gower Street with Water Street where he dug a hole and buried it. Three days later a warrant was issued for his arrest.

He was convicted and served four years of an eight-year sentence in jail. When released, he went to the laneway to recover the loot and was shocked to see that concrete steps had been constructed over his treasure. A few years later the man passed away. He never did recover the money.

THREE NEWFOUNDLANDERS FOUGHT FIFTY MEN AND WON

Newfoundlanders are known throughout the world as a hardy people. This conclusion is no doubt drawn from stories such as the one I am about to relate. This is a story which happened during the early part of the nineteenth century. It tells of the courage and cunning of three Newfoundlanders and how they outwitted and defeated fifty Frenchmen.

The brigantine *General Wolfe* set out from Carbonear in the year 1810 at a time when England and France were at war. The vessel had a full load of cod for delivery to ports on the Mediterranean. After several days at sea, the Newfoundland ship was attacked by pirates and captured.

All but three of the Newfoundlanders were ordered to go on board the enemy vessel. A group of pirates were placed on the *General Wolfe* and three Newfoundlanders were left with them to help sail the ship to France where the pirates intended to sell her cargo.

As the ship neared French waters the three Newfoundlanders, including a fifteen-year-old cabin boy, watched for an opportunity to recapture the ship. The odds of fifty to three seemed insurmountable but the trio planned and waited patiently. The mate got a gimlet and secretly bored holes in the companionways fore and aft and left some nails near each of them.

When the ship moved into French waters the pirates became a little careless, so that when the crew gathered below to eat, the Newfoundlanders put their plan into effect.

One of them slipped forward and closed the forecastle, drove nails down the gimlet holes and secured the crew in a form of prison. As all this was happening, the cabin boy seized the pistol from the pirate captain and ran to the companionway ladder.

The captain grabbed the boy by the feet but the boy tossed the gun up to the mate who was at the head of the stairs. The mate then grabbed the boy by the shoulders and pulled him to safety leaving the boy's boots in the hands of the angry pirate captain.

The three Newfoundlanders were now in full control of the ship and sailed her to Poole, England where they were highly rewarded for their deeds.

A Newfoundland Fisherman Sold into Slavery

Fifteen-year-old Joseph Pitts left the fishing grounds off Newfoundland for what he expected would be an interesting and enjoyable trip to the Canary Islands and then back to England. However, young Pitts ran into more adventure than he ever dreamed of.

Pitts set sail on the *Speedville* of Exeter, England under the command of Joe Taylor. He kept a diary of his adventures and wrote in it, "We got safe to Newfoundland, but on coming near the coast of Spain, we were overtaken by a Dutch renegade; brought to Algiers and sold into slavery." A Moslem named Mustapha, himself an owner of a pirate ship, bought the young Pitts and showed his hatred for Christians by brutally beating the boy.

Three months later Mustapha sold Pitts to a Turk named Ibraham who treated the boy well. Pitts continued as the Turk's slave for four years after which time he was sold to a Moslem named Omar. Omar also treated the boy well. He took him on a pilgrimage to the Moslem holy city of Mecca. They travelled by sea from Algiers to Alexandria and from there by caravan to Cairo and Suez. Pitts recalled in his diary that Omar treated him well and he saw Mohammed's tomb in Medina.

According to Moslem custom, Pitts was given his freedom while in the Holy City. At the time he was set free, Pitts had completed nine years of captivity and was determined to return to England as he made his way through deserts and crossed seas. No sooner had he arrived home when misfortune overtook him again. He was pressed into the British navy. While waiting to sail he sent a letter to Sir William Falkner, a Turkish merchant in London, asking for protection. Sir William came to Pitt's assistance and when the young man's background was properly represented to authorities he was released from the navy and allowed to resume his life as a British subject.

New Guinea Cannibals

Newfoundlanders have travelled all over the world and no doubt their many adventures, if ever collected and written, would fill volumes of books. One such Newfoundland adventurer during the turn of the twentieth century came in contact with a New Guinea cannibal tribe and came close to becoming the main course at a tribal dinner.

Just weeks before the confrontation with cannibals, Jim Greene signed up on a ship at St. John's harbour named the *Mambare* which was heading for Australia. As it neared Cape Nelson on the coast of New Guinea

26

the *Mambare* ran into serious trouble and went aground. The eighteen-man crew managed to escape before the ship sank but then found themselves in a situation even more life threatening than the raging sea. They were attacked by a tribe of cannibals and eleven of the ship's crew were taken prisoner. Fortunately for Greene he was not among them.

Greene and several others stayed close to the cannibal village hoping to be able to help their friends. They were not expecting to witness the cruelty and terror that followed.

For several days the tribe members participated in a wild orgy of blood and brutality. Greene watched his friends being dragged one at a time into the centre of the village, stripped, beaten and tortured. Old women and children took part in these acts sometimes allowing wild dogs to attack the dying men.

Children cut sharp sticks from trees and used them to gouge out eyes. The sailors in turn were placed in a large pot of boiling water after first being beheaded. Their heads were stuck on posts and paraded before the others who were waiting to suffer the same fate. Two of the victims after being tortured were tossed into a burning fire and roasted alive. Their half gnawed bones were thrown to the dogs and children.

Greene spent weeks in the jungle staying as close to the coast as possible. His tactic paid off and he was eventually rescued by a steamer. Greene's hair had turned snowy white by the time of his rescue. The steamer's crew tried to avenge the death of the sailors but were driven back by the savages.

GHOSTS,
THE SUPERNATURAL
AND OTHER MYSTERIES

A Fantastic Natural Phenomenon

One of the most fantastic natural phenomenons to occur in Newfoundland happened during the mid-nineteenth century when three suns appeared over this province. David King, a local fisherman described the event in his diary. He wrote, "The previous night to the apparition or whatever you want to call it, it froze very hard and the weather gave every indication of a hard frost. Very little coal was used by people and we used to go to the woods for our fuel. On the morning when the three suns appeared the wind veered to the north with snow flurries and by 10:00 a.m. a miserable day was in progress. At 11:15 the sky cleared temporarily and visible to all our population were three separate suns shining down from the heavens. Some people took this as a sign the world was going to end and the churches were filled with people *making their souls.*[1]

But then the clouds came again and the three suns were no longer visible. It got cold, very, very cold. Jim Kielley, who kept a store on Water Street put a goblet of water outside his door and in just five minutes the water was frozen solid. It got so cold that people on the roads had to take shelter in nearby houses."

[1] a local saying meaning a repentant person.

Big Blast from Outer Space

On April 3, 1978, a loud blast centred around the Bell Island area attracted international attention and an investigative visit from a group of American scientists.

The blast damaged houses and barns, killed animals, knocked a fuse box off a wall and burned out several television sets and other electrical appliances. One eyewitness to the phenomenon, Carol O'Brien, recalled "I heard a loud rumbling noise first then I saw a gigantic ball of fire two or three seconds later."

The rumbling noise was heard throughout Conception Bay and as far away as Cape Broyle. When the sound suddenly erupted Jim Bickford's telephone was blasted right off the wall and several of his chickens were killed. When news of the strange event hit the airwaves throughout Newfoundland a spokesman for Memorial University explained it might have been caused by a small meteorite hitting Earth. A MUN geologist went to the Island to investigate and discovered the blast had left two holes in the ground.

The incident attracted the attention of U.S. scientists and a team of experts were sent to Bell Island from New York and New Mexico to investigate the university's claim that the explosion had been caused by something from outer space entering the atmosphere.

The group of scientists quickly ruled out a meteor shower or a falling satellite as the cause. Another explanation rejected by the scientists was that the blast was the forerunner of an earthquake, perhaps explosive gases, escaping from the earth. Thomas Gold, a spokesman for the scientists said, "These theories have all been discounted and we come to the conclusion that it was an enormous electrical discharge called super lightning. All the evidence indicated it had to be a very powerful, though very unusual, bolt of lightning. The two holes in the earth likely occurred as the lightning grounded itself out." And so the mysterious blast episode ends there . . . well almost. The weather office records show there was absolutely no unusual atmospheric activity at anytime during that day.

A Creature Unexplained

A creature once appeared in St. John's Harbour that both frightened and astonished onlookers in their boats and along the shoreline. One of the witnesses to the strange appearance was Sir Richard Whitbourne who recorded the event in his diary. Whitbourne had a close look at the creature and for a brief period he felt sure it was going to attack him.

Whitbourne wrote in his diary:

> It came to within the length of a long pike from me and was about fifteen feet long. I was standing by the riverside in the Harbour at St. John's when it very swiftly came swimming towards me looking cheerfully at my face, like a woman. The face, eyes, nose, mouth, chin, ears and neck seemed to be beautiful and well proportioned. It had about the head many blue streaks resembling hair but it certainly was not hair.
>
> I saw it for a long time and another member of my company also saw it coming swiftly towards me. I thought it was going to spring ashore at me because I had often seen huge whales spring to great heights above the water as many other great fishes do, and so might this strange creature do to me, if I had stood still where I was.
>
> But when it saw that I moved away from it, it dived a little under water and swam away from me. It did often look back towards me so that I was able to see that its

> back and shoulders down to the middle were
> as square, white and smooth as the back of a
> man and from the middle to the hinder part
> it was pointed, in proportion something like
> a broad hooked arrow. I could not see from
> the neck to the shoulders.
> It later came to the boat and put both
> hands on the side. This frightened the crew
> and one of them struck it hard on the head
> and it fell back into the water. It disappeared
> for awhile but returned later approaching
> two boats near shore. The men in the boats
> were frightened by it and fled to land.

What was this strange creature? Some have suggested a seal, but certainly a master mariner like Whitbourne would have known a seal if he saw one. Sir Richard himself was mystified by the creature and speculated that it was a mermaid. The creature was never accurately identified and we have no other record of its sighting.

Astral Projection

Sometime ago I told a tale of the supernatural regarding Mrs. Ned Dower of Conche who returned from the dead and wondered if it had been a true case of resurrection or an unexplainable astral projection. While researching records at the Newfoundland Historical Society, I came across the personal writings of a Mr. J. W. Kinsella who interviewed Captain Ned Dower and his wife at their home and recorded their account of that often repeated story.

Kinsella's account is even more intriguing than the

one so often told all over Newfoundland where Mrs. Dower had spent three days in a coffin. It seems that version had some basis in truth but was an exaggeration of what actually happened at that time.

The Dowers were a very close couple. They had a collection of personal papers which they sometimes reviewed in private and then locked away in a metal box. On March 1, 1872, Dower set out for the seal hunt on his vessel the *Elsie*. Unknown to his wife he had taken the box of papers on board and placed it under his bunk.

Meanwhile his wife turned her house upside down looking for the box of papers and unable to find them became very despondent. She sat back in her chair and when her daughter came home she had all the appearances of being dead. Neighbours were called in and preparations began for Mrs. Dower's burial. Meanwhile Captain Dower, seventy miles away on the *Elsie* and stuck in the ice, was shocked to see his wife walk into his cabin, straight over to his bunk and remove the box of papers from underneath. She searched the box for one particular document, read it, then replaced it and left. Dower called the crew together and told them of the incident. All agreed that it was an omen that Mrs. Dower had died. They knelt to pray for her soul and for the ice to break so they could return for the funeral.

Back in Conche, as funeral arrangements were progressing, all in the household were astonished when the colour suddenly returned to Mrs. Dower's cheeks and she began to breathe slowly. She opened her eyes and said, "Oh, I'm so tired." She said she had gone a long distance pushed on by an invisible force. She said she caught up with her husband's ship and described going into his cabin to search for the box of valuable papers. When Dower arrived back and confirmed her story, one of the most unusual stories in Newfoundland history was born.

Ghost Story

Diver Dobbin of St. Mary's was a man of great courage. Even when he witnessed a strange apparition while digging for pirates' gold at Shoal Harbour he was not deterred. The others however, deserted him.

The story of buried treasure at Shoal Harbour was a well known story even in those days and Dobbin, the veteran of many such adventures, teamed up with eight men from St. John's on a treasure hunting expedition to retrieve the gold. When they arrived at the site which the map indicated held the gold, it was too dark to start work. While standing and talking about their plans to dig for the treasure they were all seized with an uncanny feeling and an unidentifiable dread. To break the spell, Dobbin grabbed a pick and started to dig. After a few minutes Captain Martin screamed and fell to the ground. When he regained consciousness, the men asked him what had frightened him and he refused to answer.

Dobbin led the men back to a nearby house where they were staying. Captain Martin went straight to bed while the others remained in the kitchen making light of the Martin incident.

Suddenly, a loud knock was heard at the door which was fastened by a wooden button inside. Before anyone could open the door, it flew open and a man came to the centre of the kitchen. He stood motionless and uttered no sound. A man named Breen passed out as did the others except Dobbin and Moran. Dobbin recalled that he was frightened but he kept calm. Then in front of the phantom figure appeared the bodies of eight men lying motionless on the floor.

Dobbin described the apparition as medium height and stoutly built. He wore a cap underneath which could be seen a mass of short black curls. He wore dark cloth pants, a blue coat cut sailor fashion square across the hips, and he disappeared as suddenly as he came. When Breen came to, his foot was on fire as it had been close to the fire. One of the men grabbed a knife and moved towards Breen to cut his clothing away while another just coming into the room thought the man was going to kill Breen and tried to wrestle the knife away.

Diver Dobbin intervened, took the knife away and put out the fire on Breen's clothing. The figure and the eight men on the floor vanished.

The treasure hunt came to an end when Captain Martin told Dobbin and the others that the ghost in the kitchen was the same ghost he had seen at the treasure site. The men pledged to leave the area and never talk about the phantom figure again. The last words Captain Martin said to Dobbin were, "The gold will have to lay there till the Day of Judgement."

THE STRANGE APPARITION AT BEAVER POND

This story deals with a strange apparition that appeared at Beaver Pond, Bonavista Bay, during the early 1900s.

The incident occurred during a fine day in June when two men from the Port Blandford area decided to spend the day hunting and fishing together. They set out on their adventure at 5:00 a.m. and two hours later had set up camp at Beaver Pond. However after several hours in the woods with little success the two became fed up with the whole idea and began to feel that this was not their lucky day.

As the evening drew near the skies darkened and an eerie feeling came over them. By now they were scared. Something strange was happening and they were not going to wait around and find out what it was. They were in the process of picking up their gear when they saw a canoe being peddled out of the mist on the lake.

Startled, the hunters stood by almost helpless as sudden fear gripped them. The canoe came closer and closer until they could finally see the person in it. It was a strange sight . . . an Indian maiden all decked out in aboriginal garb and headdress.

The hunters thought it was somebody playing a prank but they were not aware of anybody in the area or any of their friends owning a canoe and the woman was certainly not familiar to them.

As the Indian woman drew her bow the two hunters loaded their guns and fired the same time as the arrow left the bow. The arrow whizzed right by them. Their bullets did not have any affect on the native woman. When they turned around to see where the arrow had gone they saw a huge black bear falling to the ground with the arrow sticking in it. They turned to thank the Indian woman who had just saved their lives but as swiftly as she had appeared she was now vanishing into the mist on the lake. When the two returned home and told their friends and family about the incident one old gent blessed himself and said, "Oh my God." When asked what was wrong he answered that the apparition of the Indian woman in the Beaver Pond area had been seen before. Each time she appeared it was at a time of danger to someone in the area. The old-timer claimed the woman was the ghost of an Indian princess who was killed during a white man's raid on an Indian village located near Beaver Pond nearly a hundred years before.

THE MIRACLE AT FRESHWATER

One of the strangest events ever to occur in Newfoundland, and perhaps all of Canada, took place at Freshwater, near Argentia, during April 1947. Its results were carried in newspapers in Canada and the United States and both Canadian and American experts testified to its authenticity. The story begins with the move of the Wakeham family in January 1947 from Petite Forte to Freshwater, Placentia Bay. Eleven-year-old Ignatius Wakeham was given a slide by his older brother. While sliding down Freshwater Hill young Wakeham crashed into an oncoming taxi-cab and was instantly killed.

On the day of his funeral his friends from school, including several uniformed altar boys, were present at the Wakeham home awaiting the arrival of the priest and the funeral hearse. The boy's heartbroken mother asked the altar boys to stand around the coffin so she could take a last picture of her son. The altar boys accommodated Mrs. Wakeham, the picture was taken and the funeral arrangements proceeded. Up to this point nothing unusual had happened. However, a week later Mrs. Wakeham picked up her developed pictures from the photo finisher and was more than surprised when she viewed the picture she had taken of her son and the altar boys. The image of Ignatius resting in his coffin was as clear as any picture could be, but not one of the altar boys appeared in the picture. Instead, next to the coffin, looking down and smiling at the young boy was the Blessed Virgin Mary dressed in a plain flowing white robe and holding a rose in her hand. A ray of light was cast directly on the boy's face. At first Mrs. Wakeham consulted with the photo finisher and checked the possibility of a double exposure. That was quickly ruled out. Using a powerful magnifying glass, the face of the Virgin Mary could be seen even more clearly, in great detail. Experts from the American base at Argentia not only checked the miracle picture but also examined every picture from that roll of film. They were unable to find any flaw in the picture or the film used. The picture was also examined by Marshall's Studio in St. John's and again its authenticity verified. A high ranking official at the U.S. base was amazed after viewing the photo. He commented, "It's one of the most outstanding things I have ever seen."

Marshall's enlarged the picture three times its normal size and a copy was placed on display in their studio window. Thousands came to see the unusual photo. Many people felt it was a sign from heaven to comfort the grief-stricken family and perhaps strengthen the faith of others.

THE APPARITION OF ALICE

The diary of Aaron Thomas preserved at the Provincial Archives describes the area between

Springdale Street and Flower Hill as once being the most beautiful natural flower garden in the world. That area later was used as a racetrack where the local gentry spent many an enjoyable evening. It was also the site haunted for a decade by the spirit of Alice Janes who was among the city's most ardent racing enthusiasts. Alice with her Irish knit shawl and jug of brew was a fixture at the racetrack. During one of the many races there, Alice suffered a sudden heart attack and died almost instantly. The whole town showed up for her funeral and she was given a respectable send off at the old Church of England Cemetery opposite the Court House on Duckworth Street, the burial site for all denominations at that time.

A year passed and on the anniversary of her death, Margaret Walsh, who lived in a little cottage at Martin's Meadow, was being escorted through Flower Hill field by a visiting seaman. Darkness was just setting in and Margaret complained of a strange cold feeling. She asked her friend to bring her home and as they neared the end of the racetrack field they came upon a sight that sent both of them screaming across Branscombe's Street (now known as Central Street). At home Margaret described the frightening apparition she had witnessed. She said at first it seemed to be simply an old woman sitting on a rock with a jug in her hands. When the couple got close enough to see and perhaps speak to the lady, the figure slowly stood up and stared straight at them. Margaret said her eyes were burning red and her hair stood out like the whisks of a broom. The colour of her hair suddenly changed from khaki to white. Margaret recognized the visitor as the spirit of Alice Janes. When word of the apparition spread throughout town, several friends of Alice visited the racetrack and then Alice's grave to pray. While at the grave side they noticed that the marker which had been placed on their friend's grave after her burial had been removed. They searched the graveyard but couldn't find the missing cross.

The apparition continued to appear for more than a decade and usually on the anniversary of Alice's death. Then the gravedigger, while clearing some land, found the missing cross. The local priest was called and after blessing the marker replaced it on the grave. The date was July 21, the anniversary of Alice's demise. There were no further reports of apparitions after that date.

Mystery of the Phantom Ice Ship

Many of the legends and myths of Newfoundland have their origins in actual historical events. Sometimes careful research can connect a questionable story with proven facts and events to show that a legend may not after all have been the product of somebody's wild imagination. I was fortunate enough to have found myself in such a position when I traced the source of the legend of the phantom ice ship of Placentia Bay.

According to stories passed down from generation to generation, during the latter part of the nineteenth century a fisherman returning with his catch saw a very unusual sight approaching him. It was shaped like a ship but made entirely of ice. As the vessel neared, the fisherman took a closer look. He was startled by the presence of several bodies on the deck also encased in ice. Blessing himself and praying all the way, the fisherman turned his boat and headed back to Placentia as fast as he could. Needless to say, he found no believers, yet the story of the phantom ship with its entombed bodies became part of our folklore.

Recently while passing over some shipping records at the offices of the Newfoundland Historical Society, I came across the fascinating encounter of the *Flirt*, a Newfoundland cargo vessel, with an ice ship on Placentia Bay, during March 1879. The *Flirt*'s captain, Hubert Kane of St. Mary's, recorded that he noticed a dismantled vessel lying about two miles away. It was icebound. Kane said, "I took my crew and walked to the troubled ship. We took along some clothing and a little food. When we got close we noticed she was a large brig and had two stumps standing, her masts having been blown away. The name of the ship was the *Adelaide Foliquet*."

Using ropes and ice picks they boarded the ship which was covered in ice, inches thick. Near the galley door was the body of a man, face down and covered in ice. Kane added, "We had to use axes to free the body from ice. We forced our way through the ice into the forecastle and found two more bodies. We went to the cabin and found a woman lying face down on an icy floor. A short distance away was the body of a man. They were all enclosed in ice. An ebony crucifix was on the floor in the stateroom with the figure of the Redeemer sculptured in ivory. We took the bodies to the magistrate at Placentia for burial." The doomed vessel had left St. Pierre on November 16, 1878, four months earlier, with a cargo of fish for Marseilles, France.

CRIME
AND
JUSTICE

Strange Eighteenth Century Justice

The term 'mug of flip' has long disappeared from usage throughout Newfoundland. However, during the eighteenth century it was provocative enough for two Irishmen to fight to the death. Flip was a concoction of liquor, eggs and sugar which was used as a pep drink to give energy to the consumer. To suggest or order someone to drink a mug of flip was to suggest they were lacking energy, or else plain lazy.

Laurence Kneeves told his friend John Kelly he should get himself a mug of flip and before anyone knew what was happening punches were flying between Kneeves and Kelly. Kelly was beaten and strangled to death and Kneeves was taken to St. John's where he was tried for murder.

The Kneeves trial is especially interesting because of the insight it provides into Newfoundland's justice system during the eighteenth century. For example, in the absence of a doctor, medical examination of the victim was conducted by a legally appointed group of private citizens who in turn gave their findings to authorities.

At the conclusion of both the prosecution and defence cases, the judge invited jurors to ask questions. He then ordered the jury to weigh the evidence carefully stressing the importance of a fair and just decision. In the case of Kneeves he ordered the bailiff, "To keep the jury without meat, drink, fire, candle or lodging, or suffering any person to speak to them until they are agreed on their verdict." In this case the jury returned with a verdict of manslaughter in less than ninety minutes.

Punishment was swift. The judge ordered that the

following day at noon, Kneeves be brought back into the courtroom and burnt on the right hand with a hot iron marked with the letter R, a letter reserved for repeaters and murderers. Kneeves' punishment did not end there. In addition, the judge ordered that he forfeit all his goods and chattels, and then he was banished from Newfoundland with the warning that if he ever returned he would be hanged.

Anyone for a mug of flip?

Hanged for Killing a Cow

William Gilmore, a tavern owner at Quidi Vidi was not deterred by the penalty of hanging which the law required for the stealing or killing of a cow. On April 17, 1759, Gilmore persuaded two young customers of his establishment to join him in a plot to steal and slaughter a cow from a nearby farm. The two, David Williams and Richard Sutley, refused to take part in the deed at first but, with a few drinks Gilmore prodded them into accepting.

The tavern owner provided the two with a knife and hatchet and off they went to do his bidding. They found a cow grazing in a meadow near where Government House now stands on Military Road. Using the knife and axe the two killed and cut up the animal. Meanwhile, Gilmore, in preparation for the pending arrival of meat told his wife to clean out the pot. Margaret Gilmore replied defiantly, "I certainly will not. There's a full pot of chowder in that pot and we're having that for supper." Gilmore insisted she clean out the pot telling her he had invited friends for supper and wanted to serve something nice. When

Williams and Sutley arrived Gilmore helped them hide the meat in the well outside his tavern. Margaret seeing this began screaming, "You are harbouring thieves. You are disgracing me." Gilmore raised his leg and booted his wife in the stomach sending her flying across the kitchen. The following morning police constable Jim Forrester came to the Gilmore home and questioned Gilmore about a knife which was found near the remains of the dead cow. Forrester said, "If that is your knife then you are in plenty of trouble. It was used to kill a cow." Gilmore replied, "If that killed twenty cows, it's still mine."

Gilmore, Sutley and Williams were arrested and brought to trial. A twelve-man jury took only fifteen minutes to bring back a guilty verdict. The trio were sentenced to be hanged. Williams and Sutley because of their age and the fact they were enticed into the crime had their sentences commuted while Gilmore who did not participate in the killing of the cow was executed at the gallows in St. John's.

A Harbour Funeral

One of the most unusual funerals ever to take place in Newfoundland occurred on the morning of October 28, 1794, at the St. John's waterfront.

The silence of that morning was broken by the steady and morbid beating of military drums along the shoreline as a flotilla of dories, one of them carrying a flag-draped coffin, moved slowly over the harbour waters. On shore standing at attention in honour of the deceased, were three companies of Newfoundland volunteer servicemen, the entire crews of six British men-of-war and crowds of city residents.

This extraordinary funeral was being held to honour the slain Lieutenant Richard Lawry who had been murdered several days before during an ambush by a group of St. John's Irishmen. The lieutenant was an officer on the HMS *Boston*. He had angered the locals by press-ganging a group of their friends into service on the *Boston*. They waited on shore and when Lawry came ashore they ambushed him and beat him to death.

The governor felt that completion of a trial and execution of the guilty was absolutely necessary to preserve order throughout the Island. One of the suspects accepted the governor's offer of immunity in return for identifying the killers. As a result of this, Richard Power and Garrett Farrell were arrested and charged with murder. The trial and execution were swift.

They were tried on Wednesday, sentenced on Thursday, and executed on Friday. The hangings took place near Fort Townshend. Their bodies were turned over to local surgeons for dissection, which was part of the sentence for murder.

Before departing for England the governor offered a fifty pound reward for information leading to the arrest of a third man involved in the murder . . . William Barrows. However Barrows was never found.

Meanwhile, the victim Lieutenant Lawry was laid to rest at the old Church of England cemetery, opposite the present courthouse on Duckworth Street.

HANGED AT FORT TOWNSHEND

On September 1, 1809, John Pelley of Rocky Harbour, Bonne Bay, had been tried in court at St. John's and found guilty of double murder. His victims were Joe Randell and Richard Cross, both of whom had shared a hunting lodge with him at Shallow Cove.

Cross's sister, Sarah Singleton had complained to police after becoming alarmed over the disappearance of her brother and Joe Randell. Authorities organized a search for the missing men while Sarah and a neighbour, John Paine, stayed the night at Pelley's house. Early the next morning they joined in the search and finding some items of clothing belonging to her brother, Sarah cried out, "Oh God, my brother has been murdered." Paine shared her view but cautioned her saying, "Hold your tongue, Pelley is not far away and if he hears you he may come and kill us."

On their return to Rocky Harbour, Sarah and John enlisted the help of three men and returned to confront Pelley with their accusation of murder. They managed to get a confession from him in a way that would never be tolerated in our justice system of today. They built a large fire and kept forcing Pelley into it until he confessed.

Pelley was kept locked up in a private home at Bonne Bay until arrangements were completed to transfer him to St. John's for trial. While a prisoner Pelley shed some light on the double murders saying, "It all started when Randell told me to go out and cut some wood. I grumbled about it and said, 'If you don't keep quiet, I'll knock your liver out.' He came at me and I killed him with an axe." Cross was witness to the killing and said to Pelley, "You wouldn't kill me would you?" But Pelley ignored Cross's plea and axed him to death also.

Justice Tom Tremlett sentenced Pelley to be hanged. On the day of execution he was tied to a horse-drawn cart which paraded him around St. John's. The execution procession ended at Fort Townshend where a gallows had been erected. Pelley was escorted up the gallows where the masked executioner placed a white hood over his head. The crowds moved closer as the executioner dropped the noose over Pelley's head and stepped back to release the trap door. The noose tightened quickly around Pelley's neck and death was instant.

WINTON'S EARS

Religious bigotry was the cause of the barbarous attack upon Henry Winton, editor of the *Public Ledger*, a conservative St. John's newspaper. Winton, a Protestant and an outspoken critic of Catholic Bishop Fleming, was engaged in a print campaign against priests' influence in politics. On Tuesday, May 19, 1835, Winton and friend Captain Churchward set out from Carbonear to visit friends in Harbour Grace. Winton was on horseback while Churchward followed on foot.

When they neared Saddle Hill a gang of five men disguised with painted faces rushed from the woods and attacked them. They delivered a heavy blow with a stone to Winton's head causing him to fall from his horse. Churchward was grabbed by two of the attackers when he tried to pull a gun from his belt. While the captain was being restrained, Winton was lying on the ground and being repeatedly punched and kicked by the others. When they finished beating Winton they filled his ears with mud and gravel. Bewildered by all this, Winton asked if they intended to kill him. One of the attackers answered, "Hold your tongue." He then opened a clasped knife and ordered the others to hold Winton's hands. Winton closed his eyes and prayed silently. The man with the knife grasped Winton's right ear and sliced it from his head. The agonizing screaming of Winton and the protests from Captain Churchward did not deter the attackers. They then twisted his head to the left and sliced off his left ear. Winton passed out. When he recovered his vision was blurred from the blood that poured down his forehead. The captain, having been released unharmed, rushed to his companion's side and was trying to stop the bleeding. With blood streaming behind them the two made their way the mile and a half to Dr. Stirling's house at Harbour Grace. Stirling stopped the bleeding, bandaged the wounds and allowed Winton time to rest and regain his strength before returning home to St. John's. News of the brutal and merciless attack evoked a strong reaction in St. John's. The *Public Ledger* addressed an editorial to Winton stating, "Yours are the scars of honour on which every man will look with admiration."

Although friends of Winton contributed $2500 as a reward and the Newfoundland government another $1500, the crime was never solved.

Mutiny and Murder

A bungled mutiny, murder and robbery near St. Pierre led to the arrest and hanging of the small band of men who perpetrated the crimes. The story begins during October 1828 when the *Fullwood* set sail from Canada heading for England to purchase provisions. As was the custom in those days, the ship carried a full load of Spanish gold and other coins to make the necessary purchases. When the ship left port, the gold and coins had been locked in several large chests and stored below deck.

Crew members did not become aware of the treasure on board until they had been at sea for several days. They banded together, mutinied, stabbed the captain and officers to death and took control of the ship. In their haste to steal the gold the gang overlooked an important aspect of the mutiny; they had no one among them who could navigate a ship.

Between St. Pierre and Miquelon there is a stretch of sand, sometimes slightly covered by water, known as "the dunes," where many vessels have shipwrecked. With no one to navigate, the *Fullwood* sailed straight into the dunes and was itself wrecked. The ship was sinking faster than the men could get the gold off and in desperation they tied together some lifeboat oars to make a raft to carry the last of the gold chests. The raft broke open and the chests sank beneath the sea.

French authorities on St. Pierre investigated the sinking and discovered that mutiny, murder and robbery had led to it. The mutineers were rounded up by the French police and sent to military authorities in Newfoundland. From here they were taken to London under guard where they were tried and executed at a public hanging near the Old Bailey courthouse.

Many attempts were made to find the sunken gold. During the 1970s a resident of St. Pierre, Emilien Parrot, told a story which shed some light on the whereabouts of the hidden fortune. Parrot recalled that her uncle, while on a trouting trip, found a birch wall protruding from a sandy embankment. He dug at the site and found a quantity of gold. He kept his discovery secret and quietly took the gold to the Canadian mainland, changed it to French money and returned to St. Pierre where he built himself an expensive home and furnished it lavishly. Emilien had two paintings which were taken from her uncle's home and which had been purchased with the money obtained from the sale of the *Fullwood*'s gold.

MASS MURDERERS DETECTED BY A NEWFOUNDLANDER

When a group of wealthy Dutch people decided to pick up their roots and move to the American West, they chartered the ship SS *Commerskie*, turned their fortunes over to the captain for safekeeping and set out on what was to be one of the most bizarre stories in Newfoundland's history. Just before leaving port a beautiful young girl was forced by her family to marry one of the wealthy men going on the expedition to the New World. She was most unhappy until she met and fell in love with the ship's captain, himself a married man.

Near Cape Race tragedy struck the *Commerskie*, and in the darkness of night the vessel sank to the bottom of the ocean. The captain, however, his wife and eight crew members turned up safely at Bigley's Cove the next morning. He informed authorities that the ship had struck a rock and sunk taking with her to the bottom of the ocean seventy-four men and women who were unable to escape. The survivors returned to England on the first ship out of Burin. Then the rumours started. People wondered why none of the bodies had washed ashore. Was the lady with the captain really his wife?

At the time, Thomas David Dobbin of St. Mary's was making a name for himself as a pioneer of the recently invented diver's suit. By the time he arrived at Burin he had already gone to the ocean floor in the suit and recovered thousands of dollars in treasure. When he learned of the recent sinking at Silver's Cove he decided to take a look to see if there was anything worth salvaging. What he found shocked people throughout the world.

As Dobbin moved slowly through the murky waters on deck of the sunken ship he couldn't believe what he was seeing. There in front of him was a woman with long blond hair, a blue coat and a red dress floating about in the water as though she was dancing. Nearby stood four men with their backs to the rail. Then he saw the rope that held her hands to the ratline of the main mast. The four men had their hands bound to the deck rails. Recalling the rumours he had heard in Burin, Dobbin surfaced, and advised the people above of his discovery and went below again. This time the scene was even more macabre. The other sixty-nine men and women had been locked in their cabins and the doors nailed shut. The victims were in every possible position, some kneeling in prayer, some huddling in corners and others showing agony-filled eyes.

Authorities sent a full report to England. At the sensational trial that followed, it was learned that the captain had plotted the mass murder and had the support of eight of the crew members and the unhappy girl who fell in love with him. They selected Cape Race because of its deep waters and history of shipwrecks. The captain had included his wife among those to be murdered and after the deed was done, passed the young girl off as his wife. The seventy-four murdered victims were buried near Cape Race at a place called the Plantation. The murderers were hanged with the exception of the girl who spent the rest of her life in prison.

Blamed for Mass Murder

Captain Rideout's schooner was shipwrecked during 1874 near Bay of Islands. When rescuers got to the vessel there was evidence that some, if not all of the crew, had managed to get ashore. There were no bodies to be found so it was assumed they had headed inland looking for help.

Three years later there was still no sign of the survivors and rumours began to circulate around the island. These rumours ended up in local newspapers and authorities launched an investigation. The governor ordered Captain Erskine of the *Eclipse* to go to the west coast to investigate the stories, and if enough evidence was found, to make an arrest.

According to reports in the Newfoundland and Nova Scotia press there had been wholesale murder of the ship's crew by a gang headed by the Benoit brothers from Newfoundland's west coast. The press reported that Captain Rideout had engaged Francois, Xavier and Gil Benoit to guide them to the nearest community. When the Benoits learned that the captain was carrying a large sum of money they shot him and killed all his crew. Reports said they cut a hole in the ice and shoved the bodies down into the water.

An old man named Jocko lived nearby and the Benoits believing he might report what he had seen, offered him a share of the stolen fortune to keep quiet.

When Erskine set out to conduct his investigation, interest in the mystery was so high that Supreme Court Justice Lilly joined him on the trip. Interest heightened when the press reported that old Jocko was on his deathbed and ready to confess. However, when Erskine and Lilly found Jocko he was in good health and claimed he knew nothing of Rideout, his crew or any mass murder. The three Benoits were arrested and placed in jail at Channel. The investigation continued and no evidence was found. Meanwhile, one of the brothers died in prison and there was a public outcry that the brothers should not have been held unless there had been sufficient proof to charge them in court.

The Crown was unable to bring charges against the Benoits due to lack of evidence and the two surviving brothers were released. The press which had a field day speculating on the mass murder now switched to attacking Erskine and Lilly for not conducting a proper investigation and for holding innocent men under arrest. Letters to the editor in the local newspapers strongly condemned Erskine and Lilly also. One letter signed by 'Verax' stated, "No person could exonerate Captain Erskine of the HMS *Eclipse*, nor Judge Lilly nor Inspector McCarty for what they had done to the Benoits. The writer said that Captain Erskine arrested "these poor fellows, subjecting them to hardships that would be harsh were they even condemned by a jury of their peers." He added that Erskine should have investigated more fully and then would have realized that there were no grounds for arrest.

The Victim of the Boston Slasher

Three police departments, a top U.S. detective and a snooping Boston newspaper reporter competed against each other in an intense effort to discover the identity of the person who murdered Annie Mullins of Blackmarsh Road, St. John's. The twenty-five-year-old Annie was found in Boston on the morning of March 28, 1908, with two deep gashes in her throat. The Mullins murder attracted national attention in the United States because Annie was employed by a prominent Harvard University professor. The competitors in the investigation refused to cooperate with each other and accused the other of bungling the case. There were several leads, a number of suspects and each investigator seemed to be trying to prove that his own suspect was the slasher.

A year passed and the investigations failed to lead to any arrest. A second inquest was held and at its conclusion it seemed a solution would never be found to the mystery. Then a strange and unusual event took place that led to the arrest and conviction of the slasher.

Peter Delorey and Jim Manter who lived near the murder site with Pete's aunt, Liz Delorey, indicated on the morning Annie's body was found that they knew something about the crime. Aunt Liz decided against telling police because the penalty for murder was the electric chair. At the time of the second inquest, Peter and Jim were arguing with Aunt Liz over wages. Upset by Liz's refusal to increase their pay, the two packed their bags and left. However, before leaving they committed an act which angered Aunt Liz so much that she immediately went to the police and implicated her nephew and his friend in the Mullins murder. The act which prodded Aunt Liz into action was the cutting off of her cow's tail by the departing duo.

Liz later told police, "I had to report them. The ghost of Annie Mullins was always there. She haunted me and tormented me until I couldn't take anymore. Her ghost seemed always hovering over me and I got so that I couldn't go around the corner without seeing her."

Peter Delorey confessed to taking part in the killing. He told police that they enticed the girl into a field near her home and when she resisted their advances Jim Manter, a Greek immigrant, pulled a knife and cut her throat.

A spectacular trial followed with Greek citizens of Boston collecting over $5,000 to aid in Manter's defence. The defence lawyers called in medical experts to raise the possibility that Annie Mullins may have committed suicide. During the trial it was disclosed that the two defendants had stood with hundreds of spectators on the morning when police were removing the victim's body from the field.

The jury, after considering the evidence presented, found Delorey and Manter guilty of murder. Peter Delorey was sentenced to twenty years in prison while Jim Manter, the slasher, got life.

THE CHINESE MURDERS

The triple slaying of three Chinese laundrymen on Carter's Hill in 1922 was the most cold-blooded murder to happen in Newfoundland since 1872, when Patrick Geehan murdered his wife and brother-in-law.

A dispute over wages, working conditions and family hostilities that were carried over from China, led to the murders of the owners of the Jim Lee Laundry on Carter's Hill. Wo Fen Game, an employee at the laundry, was angered because one of the owners, Hong Loen, was threatening to fire him and throw him out on the street. Game could not speak English and he viewed this action as a death sentence. He felt no one else would hire him because he couldn't speak English, and other Chinese businessmen would not assist him because they felt it would offend the Jim Lee Laundry owners who had paid to bring Wo Fen into the country.

While this dispute was building, Hong Loen told Wo Fen that he would die sooner or later and that Hong Wing of the Hop Wah Laundry on Casey Street intended to kill him. Wing, according to Ho Kim Hi, was determined to kill Wo Fen because of a dispute between the two families that had been going on for decades back in China.

Wo Fen sought the help of his friend Charlie Fong, an operator of a Water Street restaurant. Fong met with Hong Loen and tried to persuade him not to fire Wo Fen Game. His efforts nevertheless failed.

When told of this, Wo Fen Game went to the Royal Stores on Water Street, purchased a gun and that evening shot and killed Ho Kim Hi, Hong Loen and So Ho Kai. He then went to the Hop Wah Laundry and shot Hong Wing. Fortunately, Wing was only wounded. Wo Fen then walked across the street to the top of Barron Street, raised the gun to his own head and with his hand trembling, fired. He was taken to the General Hospital. Upon recovery he was arrested and tried for murder. During the trial he had to be gagged, tied and held at the back of the courtroom.

While at Her Majesty's Penitentiary he got hold of a gun and made an unsuccessful attempt to escape. At 8:00 a.m. on the morning of December 16, 1922, Wo Fen Game was escorted to the gallows in the prison yard. When he saw the six-foot-tall executioner approach him dressed in an overcoat with a woolen hat partially covering his face, his whole body began to tremble. The execution was swift and the prisoner died instantly at 8:09 a.m.

RUM RUNNING NEWFOUNDLANDERS

It was the era of Al Capone, and Prohibition was making rum-running a profitable but dangerous business. Captain Bill Cluett and his brother Alf, both of St. John's, were attracted to the rum-running trade by the high profits, excitement and risk attached to it. They faced danger not only from the U.S. Coast Guard but also from a large gangster syndicate connected with Capone which operated thirty-seven vessels out of New England.

Yet in spite of the constant risks, the Cluetts managed to survive in the business for more than five years, without having any confrontations with either the law or the gangsters. However on the morning of January 25, 1931, their luck ran out. A U.S. Coast Guard cutter pulled alongside the *Josephine K* and without any warning opened fire on the slow moving vessel. The first shot went across the bow while the second crashed through the wheelhouse window and penetrated the chest of Captain Bill Cluett. Cluett dropped to the floor as his ship was brought to a stop.

In minutes the Coast Guard crew stormed aboard the *Josephine K* with their weapons loaded and ready to fire. The fifteen-man crew, including four Newfoundlanders, were all placed under arrest and taken to New York where they were imprisoned. Cluett survived the trip but died shortly after being admitted into a New York hospital.

Meanwhile, Alf Cluett was released on bail and joined other family members from Newfoundland on a trip to Lunenburg, Nova Scotia to attend funeral services for his deceased brother, whose wife and children resided there.

The incident captured newspaper headlines around the world and within hours of Cluett's death, the British and Canadian governments expressed grave concerns over the killing and claimed the incident occurred outside the twelve mile limit. The American government responded by ordering an immediate enquiry into the incident.

Reverend E. Ryder, speaking at the victim's funeral service, described Cluett as a good husband and father, a good friend and a master mariner. He told the gathering that Cluett's death was nothing less than murder on the high seas. He said it was one of the inevitable tragedies that follows the hypocrisy of Prohibition.

Back in St. John's the Cluetts spoke openly of their involvement in rum-running. Mrs. Cluett said she was proud of her son but wanted him to retire from the illegal trade. Alf had other ideas. He indicated he would resume his activities because he loved the excitement attached to it. The U.S. government enquiry into the incident exonerated the Coast Guard. Public criticism of the enquiry failed to change anything and the shooting of Bill Cluett was described as an accidental shooting that occurred while the Coast Guard was effecting a legal arrest.

Riot on Water Street

It took the combined efforts of the Newfoundland Constabulary and British military police to stop a riot outside a Water Street cafe started by three British seamen. As darkness set in over the city on Christmas Day 1942, three British seamen looking for a place to go, were attracted to the Imperial Cafe on Water Street, where the Chinese owners were celebrating the Christmas holidays with friends.

When they approached the door the manager, visible through the window, raised his hand and shook his head to indicate the place was closed. The British sailors misinterpreted this gesture and took it as an insult. One of them stood back, raised his foot and delivered a hard kick to the door which sent it swinging wide open. As the seamen forced their way in, the Chinese occupants fought back and during the struggle one of the sailors was struck over the head with a bottle. The sailors retreated to their ship at St. John's harbour.

While the Chinese made repairs to the door the sailors incited their shipmates by telling them how they had been the victims of an unprovoked attack. Feeling the incident was as much an insult to the Royal Navy as to the victims, the crew left the ship and began to march towards the cafe. In minutes a full ship's company of 150 sailors were storming down Water Street to avenge their honour.

The cafe manager couldn't believe his eyes when

he looked out the window and saw the horde of British sailors marching angrily towards the Imperial Cafe. The man shouted something in Chinese causing the others to scatter in all directions. Some ran out the back door while others locked themselves in an upstairs room.

The sailors kicked open the door knocking it off its hinges, beat out windows, tossed furniture into the street and overturned the counter. Grabbing food from the fridge and tables they painted the walls and ceilings with everything from rice to coconut cream pie and topped this off by pouring soup and flour over the floors. When the police and British patrols arrived the place was in shambles. The men were ordered back to their ships and to remain on board until further notice. Meanwhile, local authorities fearing other Chinese establishments might be attacked cautioned the Chinese community to stay off the streets. There was no further trouble and the British were satisfied they had gotten revenge.

WAR, BATTLES
AND
MILITARY HEROES

NEWFOUNDLAND
COURAGE AND INGENUITY

Newfoundlanders are known throughout the world for their courage, independence and ingenuity, traditions no doubt set and established by men like John Earle of Little Bell Island. Earle, his wife and three children were the only inhabitants of Little Bell Island when the French attacked and took possession of St. John's in 1696. That year the French had set out in another of their efforts to drive the English out of Newfoundland. Earle realized that it would only be a matter of weeks before the French would invade Bell Island and then Little Bell Island. Earle was determined to make a stand against the French even though the odds were strongly against him. One advantage he had was that there was only one landing spot on the island, which was located on a beach. It was on this beach that Earle planned to make his stand. He carted a small cannon down the slope and placed it in position. He then made a dozen or more wooden cutouts that resembled soldiers. Earle constructed a fortress along the beach and placed the wooden soldiers at strategic points along the front of the fortress. He then placed a musket with each figure. When he ran out of muskets he used wooden sticks carved to resemble rifles.

On January 19, 1697, the French left Portugal Cove using two longboats to ferry their troops. Earle waited patiently and when the first barge moved into the cove he held his fire until it got close enough, then fired his cannon sinking the French troop carrier. While the other soldiers were pulling their comrades from the water, Earle ran from wooden soldier to wooden soldier firing a rifle from each position. The unexpected resistance on the island convinced the French they were up against a well-trained fighting unit and they immediately retreated.

Little Bell Island, thanks to the determination and cleverness of John Earle, was the only settlement in Conception Bay not destroyed by the French that year. John Earle and his family knelt and gave thanks to God for their deliverance from the French threat. The Earle family bible is preserved at the Newfoundland Museum.

THE ONLY BRITISH ADMIRAL EVER LEGALLY EXECUTED

John Byng served as governor of Newfoundland during the mid-eighteenth century and later he became an admiral in the British navy. He is best remembered in history as the only British admiral ever legally executed. In 1962, publishers McClelland and Stewart released the book *At 12 Mr. Byng Was Shot*, by Arthur Dudley Pope, chronicling the tragic story of the former Newfoundland governor.

The incident leading to the court-martial and execution of Byng began when he commanded a small, undermanned and ill-equipped naval fleet in the Mediterranean Battle of Majorca. Byng put up a good battle and the French retreated. However, the French claimed they had defeated Byng. British authorities responded by ordering Byng's court-martial for what they termed as his not doing enough in the battle.

Evidence at the court-martial was flimsy and Byng was cleared of all suggestions of cowardice. Not doing

enough in battle was not an offence, yet Byng was pro-
nounced guilty and sentenced to be shot. The man
pronouncing the death sentence was Captain Thomas
Smith, himself a former governor of Newfoundland.

At noon on March 14, 1757, Byng found himself
kneeling on a red cushion on the quarter deck of the
HMS *Monarch*. He held a white handkerchief in each
hand. He tied one around his head to cover his eyes.
The second he held high with one hand, waited a
moment or two and then dropped it. This was the signal for the marine firing squad, standing with their
guns just two feet from Byng's chest, to fire. Pope in
his book characterized the execution as, "One of the
most cold-blooded and cynical acts of judicial murder
in the whole of British history."

Oh yes, this tragic incident had one more connec-
tion with Newfoundland. The captain of the *Monarch*,
George Rodney, was also a former governor of
Newfoundland.

CARTER'S NAVY

Newfoundland history is full of accounts of famous
battles involving the British navy and the French navy
but who ever heard of Carter's navy? Carter's navy,
organized by fishermen of the Southern Shore, were
courageous and valiant fighters and played a major
role in driving the French out of Newfoundland.
Carter's navy had a garrison at the entrance to
Ferryland harbour and succeeded in fighting off
pirate, French and Dutch attacks.

Their most outstanding achievement was the
major part played in the Battle of Signal Hill in 1762.

During that year England had left Newfoundland poorly defended. Concerned over the threat of a French invasion, local merchants equipped a brig with guns and ammunition at their own expense, and gave the command to John Neil. When French intelligence learned of the weak defence in St. John's, they immediately set the wheels in motion for an invasion. On June 24, 1762, they landed their forces at Bay Bulls and marched overland through a narrow wooded path until they arrived at St. John's. The French experienced little trouble in capturing the sixty-three soldiers and offices at the city garrison. They also took possession of the HMS *Granot*, the only British warship then in St. John's harbour. Once in control of St. John's, the French sent troops to Conception Bay and Trinity Bay with orders to burn all houses and kill any residents showing resistance. The French were in control and it seemed as though the British had little chance of regaining the old colony.

Governor Grave sent a request for help to Admiral Colville at Halifax. Colville teamed up with Sir Jeffery Amherst and with a combined force of 800 highlanders and 200 infantryman set sail for St. John's. Meanwhile, the gallant fishermen of the Southern Shore were secretly putting together their own civilian navy. Robert Clarke and Mr. Brooks organized the effort and enlisted volunteers from Toad's Cove to Renews. Fishermen turned over their schooners and western boats and had them converted into row-galleys, well armed with guns. Carter was made commodore and Brooks was designated captain of the squadron.

Carter's navy cooperated with the British forces in planning strategy to recapture St. John's. Under cover of darkness, Carter's navy rowed past St. John's to

Torbay. As a diversion, Lord Colville landed his fleet at Quidi Vidi. The French spotted them and sent wave after wave of soldiers down the hill to fight the British. Unexpectedly for the French, Carter's men arrived on the scene approaching from the river entering Quidi Vidi. This inspired the British fighter Lieutenant Shuley who shouted, "Advance on Signal Hill, do or die." In less than an hour the French were defeated and the British regained control of the old colony. Captain McDonald and twenty-one soldiers were killed during the battle.

TWO BELL ISLANDERS WHO FOUGHT FOR NAPOLEON

When Napoleon set out on his conquest of Europe he was supported by his vast French army and two Bell Islanders. Thomas and Daniel Dwyer ended up in France fighting on the side of Emperor Napoleon but not of their own free will. The Dwyer boys were fishing in waters near Portugal Cove when a heavy fog moved in over the area. The two decided to anchor down for a few hours until the fog lifted.

As the fog receded the Dwyers were astonished to see a large French frigate with its guns aimed at them less than a hundred yards away. The French ship was part of a fleet under the command of Admiral Richery which was sent out to attack St. John's, but failed in its mission due to the protection given the city by The Narrows. The Dwyers started to row as fast as they could but the French fired a shot right over their bow. The Bell Islanders stopped and heard a French accented voice ask, "Who are you?"

Tom Dwyer stood up and answered, "Two sons of a Stradbully, County Waterford Irishman," and shook his fist at the French.

The French officers laughed and took the two Dwyers captive. They were taken to the great French naval base in the Mediterranean near Toulan. Daniel died in Paris and Tom returned to Bell Island following the Napoleonic Wars.

Newfoundlanders at a Famous Naval Battle

Twenty-two Newfoundlanders took part in the epic naval battle of the War of 1812 fought between the *Shannon* and the *Chesapeake*! The *Chesapeake* was the pride of the American navy and had been ordered from Washington to stop British ships from going up the St. Lawrence river.

However, before the vessel could carry out its orders, she ran into the *Shannon* which had among its crew twenty-two Newfoundlanders, and in sixteen minutes flat the pride of the U.S. Navy was in shambles. The Newfoundlanders' adventure began on December 5, 1812, from Little Bay, Notre Dame Bay, when the men joined the crew of the brig *Duck*, owned by Newman and Company. The ship set out for Portugal with a cargo of fish it intended exchanging for a cargo of wine.

On the seventeenth day at sea the *Duck* was captured by the French, its cargo dumped and then allowed to sail on to Portugal. But the Newfoundlanders' troubles were far from over. A few days later they were taken prisoners by Captain

Plumer of the U.S. Navy. Then a British privateer under the command of Sir John Sherbrooke confronted the Americans in battle and rescued the twenty-two Newfoundlanders.

Sherbrooke delivered the Newfoundlanders to the famous HMS *Shannon* which was already short of crew members. The *Shannon*, stationed at Boston, was under orders to intercept all craft coming out of that harbour and other New England ports.

Meanwhile the *Chesapeake* had just been refitted at Boston and, under the command of Captain Lawrence, was unknowingly heading towards a confrontation with the *Shannon*. When the *Chesapeake* was sighted by the *Shannon*, a challenge was issued to the Americans, which was accepted.

The *Chesapeake* had thirty-eight guns while the *Shannon* had forty-four. In addition, the *Shannon* was better handled and her fire was more accurate and deadly. She also had twenty-two fighting Newfoundlanders on board.

In just sixteen minutes the *Chesapeake* was a wreck and her commander fatally wounded. As Captain Lawrence was carried below he made the famous battle cry that has since been the watchword of the American navy, "Don't give up the ship." Minutes later Lawrence was dead and the *Chesapeake* crew surrendered.

The official naval report mentioned the twenty-two Newfoundlanders stating they did their work manfully in a celebrated fight. The Newfoundlanders won glory for their country and their employers, Newman and Company, which were given the right to fly the white, or naval, ensign over their Newfoundland establishment.

THE NEWFOUNDLANDER WHO MADE ABRAHAM LINCOLN PROUD

When the Union forces of Abraham Lincoln developed a plan to close the final port on the eastern seaboard still under Confederate control, a young Newfoundlander was to play a heroic part in the daring and dangerous task.

As the American Civil War neared its end, only one port remained under Confederate control and that was Wilmington, North Carolina. It was through this port that the Confederates communicated with the outside world and obtained all the supplies and provisions they needed. President Lincoln concluded that it was impossible for his forces to close the port without the cooperation of the army but the army had its hands full in other battles waging throughout the South.

The Union forces' top miliary strategists developed a plan to knock out the seventy-five-gun battery which guarded Wilmington Harbour. To do this they would use 150 tonnes of dynamite which they planned on having towed to the target during the darkness of night and left there to explode. The dynamite boat was fitted for the mission at Beaufort, North Carolina. Fuses were carefully laid to assure a simultaneous explosion to be caused by a combination of candles and a system of clockwork.

When volunteers for the mission were sought only eight men stepped forward. One of them was John Neil, a native of St. John's.

On the night of the mission the men stripped to the waist and blackened themselves to reduce the chances of detection. Slowly the dynamite-laden vessel crept towards its objective. There was a great deal of tension among the men because at anytime the guns on shore could blast them out of the water. Neil's men succeeded in placing the ship at its target point. They then set the dynamite to go off and jumped into the water for the treacherous quarter of a mile swim back to their home vessel. Two hours passed before there was any explosion and while it did not completely destroy the battery as hoped, it set the final hours of the Civil War in motion.

At the sound of the explosion the Union army began the bombardment of Wilmington and in less than three hours succeeded in taking control of the port. Lincoln was elated and John Neil, the little fellow from Victoria Street in St. John's, was awarded the Congressional Medal of Honor by the president.

FAMOUS AMERICAN GENERAL WITH A NEWFOUNDLAND CONNECTION

General Thomas Francis Meagher, a famous general during the U.S. Civil War, was the son of a Water Street merchant who operated in Newfoundland during the early nineteenth century.

Meagher was actually born at Waterford, Ireland in 1823, after his father's business in Newfoundland had collapsed and the family returned to Ireland. At the age of twenty-five he showed signs of leadership ability when he became one of a five member directorate of the Young Irish Federation. He travelled throughout Ireland with other group leaders inciting revolt against British rule. His association with the federation was short lived and in less than a year he had been captured and imprisoned by the British. The penalty for treason was execution and that was the sentence the court passed on young Meagher. However, because of his youth, that sentence was commuted to life imprisonment and he was sent to the prison colony in Australia, called Van Dieman's Land, but better known as Tasmania.

Six years later he escaped from the island and made his way to New York to begin his outstanding career as a military man. At first he travelled throughout New York lecturing on the injustices of the British against Ireland and he enrolled in university to study law. By 1855, at the age of thirty-two he had become a lawyer, and by then was a noted leader among the Irish of New York state. He also became editor of several Irish newspapers.

When civil war broke out he joined the military and became captain of the illustrious Fighting 69th Regiment. His first battle was at the famous Battle of Bull Run. At the age of thirty-nine he was promoted to the rank of brigadier general of the Irish Brigade of the Union Forces. Meagher fought many battles and was wounded and near death on several occasions. In 1863 he resigned but was recalled to duty within a year after his resignation.

General Meagher was present when President Abraham Lincoln made his famous Gettysburg Address. At the end of the Civil War, Lincoln appointed him as secretary of Montana territory and he later served as governor of Montana. On July 1, 1867, Meagher accidentally drowned in the Missouri River near Fort Brenton. Speculation was rampant that he had been the victim of foul play but that was never proven.

According to the records of Archbishop Howley, General Meagher's older brother Patrick became the first Newfoundlander to be ordained to the priesthood of the Roman Catholic church.

Newfoundland's Great Indian Fighter

The name Michael McCarthy is recorded in U.S. military history as one of the most courageous and outstanding cavalry men of the nineteenth century. McCarthy, who emigrated from his Gower Street home in St. John's to the United States, displayed heroism that earned him the Congressional Medal of Honor and promotion to Captain of the Presidential Guard at the White House.

As a sergeant in the cavalry, McCarthy was a veteran of many battles but none were so fierce as the savage battle his troop waged with the Nez Percé Indians of Idaho. This tribe, tired of being forced from reservation to reservation by government authorities had decided to fight back. Led by their chief, Looking Glass, the Nez Percé attacked bands of U.S. settlers and then headed northeast towards Montana.

Military leaders felt that a show of strength would be enough to force the Indians into submission. However, they did not consider the Nez Percé determination to fight back. When McCarthy's ninety man troop under the command of Captain G. Perry set out on their mission, they carried only forty rounds of ammunition for their single carbine and twelve bullets for each pistol.

McCarthy caught up with the Indians at White Bird Canyon, where his cavalry unit was outnumbered eight to one. Perry demanded that the Indians surrender. However, Looking Glass responded by insisting his tribe would fight to the last man. A battle was inevitable. The result was the Battle of White Bird Canyon fought on June 17, 1877.

Perry ordered McCarthy to take a detail of six men to an elevated position to the right of the attacking Indians and hold it at all costs. Before Perry could complete his battle preparations the Indians burst forward, yelling, screaming, filling the air with hideous howls and showers of bullets. Realizing the futility of the cavalry position, Perry ordered a retreat.

McCarthy, seeing the change in tactics from his stand inside Indian lines, fought his way out and assisted his captain in controlling the movement of the troops. When Perry's forces were on high ground and out of harm's way, McCarthy fought his way back through Indian lines to rescue his own stranded detail. Records at the Library of Congress in Washington say McCarthy fought fiercer than any Indian.

McCarthy took his band of six and waged a battle through Indian lines. Troops watching the battle from the hills were sickened at the massacre going on below them but cheered when they saw McCarthy burst through the Indian lines, losing only two of his men. Although the U.S. Cavalry was defeated that day, Michael McCarthy of St. John's earned a place in U.S. military history. He was awarded the Congressional Medal of Honor and promoted to Captain of the Presidential Guard at the White House.

LITTLE KNOWN WAR HEROES

Tommy Ricketts is well remembered in Newfoundland history for his wartime heroism which earned him the Victoria Cross. Not as well known are two other Newfoundlanders, Private John Croak of Little Bay and Henry Rideout of Pilley's Island, also outstanding war heroes.

During World War I, Henry George Rideout penetrated enemy lines armed only with an axe and proceeded to cut off German artillery communications. Thousands of Canadian and British troops had been pinned down by German fire and Rideout's action succeeded in confusing the enemy and freeing his fellow infantrymen to escape the German hold, and launch their own successful offensive. Rideout, the son of Reuben and Annie Rideout of Notre Dame Bay, was awarded the Serbian Medal of Valour for the act. Rideout passed away at Hamilton, Ontario in 1937.

Private John Croak earned his Victoria Cross near Amiens, France during one of the final Allied offences of World War I. On August 9, 1918, Croak's section had penetrated enemy lines and he found himself cut off and alone in a wooded area. Suddenly he came under fire from a machine gun post near the edge of the woods. Instead of retreating, and with complete disregard for his own safety, Croak held his ground and tossed grenades into the machine gun nest. He then charged the Germans in a gunfire exchange that resulted in his being wounded in the right shoulder. Nevertheless, he killed several Germans and took the rest prisoner. Single-handedly he took the prisoners back to his section. No sooner had he joined the group when another spray of machine gunfire erupted sending the soldiers scattering for cover. Although still bleeding from his wound, Croak started to run towards the source of the gunfire using his own gun as he moved closer and closer to the enemy. Inspired by Croak's heroism other soldiers began to follow. This time three machine gun posts were destroyed and another group of German soldiers taken prisoner. Croak passed away that night from the wounds received during his heroic efforts. He was laid to rest at the British cemetery in Hangard Woods, France.

PICKERSGILL

Interrogation by Hitler's Gestapo, according to Allied intelligence experts, was something no human being could face without terror. Frank Pickersgill, brother of former federal cabinet minister and member of Parliament for Bonavista, Jack Pickersgill, suffered through the ordeal of a Gestapo interrogation. In so doing, he displayed tenacity, valour and loyalty that ranks him among the most courageous men in Canadian history.

Pickersgill and John McAlister were two Canadian intelligence agents parachuted into German-occupied France on June 16, 1943. They had spent months undergoing special training for their mission which was to set up a radio station behind enemy lines to relay information on German activity to the Allies. Their training briefed them on Gestapo interrogation methods. On the day of the duo's scheduled time to start their dangerous mission, the Allies were advised that German security forces were swarming the target area which increased the possibility of being captured.

Undaunted by the new dangers, McAlister and Pickersgill went through with their assignment. As they neared LeMans they were picked up in a car by their French contact, forty-seven-year-old Yvonne Rudalatt. As they neared Paris they ran into a road-block. They passed the brief inspection and were ready to move on when a Gestapo officer requested another look at their papers. Yvonne suspected the officer was onto them and she stepped on the gas. The Gestapo gave chase and used their gun power to force the escaping car to stop. Yvonne fell from the vehicle wounded. When two German guards started beating her with their gun butts she pulled a revolver and killed them both. She was then taken to prison, tortured and eventually executed in a gas chamber at Belsen prison.

Only one connection with the Allied intelligence network now operated in France and the Gestapo did their utmost to persuade Pickersgill and McAlister to tell them of that connection and the names of others involved with the spy network. Half starved and bleeding, Pickersgill remained tight lipped. When the opportunity presented itself, Pickersgill seized a bottle, broke the neck and jabbed it into the face of one of the Gestapo interrogators. The jab cut the officer's jugular vein and killed him. Pickersgill jumped through a window but was stopped by a hail of German bullets. He was seriously wounded and was once more reintroduced to the terror of the Gestapo. Pickersgill and McAlister were taken to a concentration camp and hung from a butcher's hook where the Gestapo allowed them to die slowly by strangulation against the crematorium walls. Frank Pickersgill was twenty-nine years old at the time of his death in 1944 at Buchenwald prison.

NAZI ATTACK ON BELL ISLAND

World War II was brought right to the doorstep of Newfoundland for the first time on September 5, 1942, when a Nazi U-boat attacked and sunk two iron ore carriers which had been anchored between Little Bell Island and Lance Cove, waiting to join an overseas convoy. The waters in Conception Bay were calm and the skies overcast when Commander Rolf Rüggeberg manoeuvred his U-boat 513 beneath the water's surface to a position directly in line with the ore carrier *Lord Strathcona*. The commander ordered his men to torpedo the ore carrier but when they pulled the switch nothing happened. The crew had forgotten to set the battery from charge to fire. The torpedoes left their tubes but sank. The U-boat then surfaced and was spotted by the Newfoundland cutter *Evelyn B* moving near the southwest corner of Kelly's Island heading out to sea.

At a range of fifteen hundred yards the *Evelyn B* opened fire and the shell passed near the U-boat's periscope. The sub dived and retaliated by firing two torpedoes which struck and sank the ore carrier SS *Saganaga* nearby. The *Evelyn B* and the Free French ship PLM 27 made an effort to get out of the harbour. Because of shallow waters the U-boat could not move with her accustomed ease and when the *Lord Strathcona* swung around suddenly, it struck the U-boat's tower forcing her into the mud of the shallow harbour. Once more the U-boat sent off two torpedoes and this time they sent the *Lord Strathcona* to the bottom. The Germans could not reload the torpedoes fast enough and as they escaped out of Conception Bay they missed a final opportunity to sink the *Evelyn B*.

Thirty people died on the *Saganaga*, however the *Strathcona*'s crew had abandoned ship when they saw how the battle shaping up. The captain of the *Evelyn B* was given a special award for bravery for sticking with his ship and fighting off the U-boat attack. On November 2 two more ships were attacked by a Nazi U-boat and the wharf at Bell Island was blown to pieces with some of it landing two hundred feet away.

THE WAR ON OUR DOORSTEPS

On November 2, 1942, at 3:30 a.m., a German U-boat torpedoed the SS *Rose Castle* and the Free French ship PLM *27*, killing forty men and destroying the wharf on Bell Island. This occurred just two months after a German U-boat 513 sank two ore carriers near Lance Cove in broad daylight. The PLM 27 was the same vessel that joined with the *Evelyn B* in fighting off the Germans during the August attack.

At the time of this tragedy most of the crew of both ships were asleep. The *Rose Castle* was owned by Dominion Steel and commanded by William J. McDonald. The PLM 27 was captained by J. B. Chance and owned by the Ministry of War Transport in London and manned by the Free French. The *Rose Castle* was anchored between the Scotia Pier and Lance Cove. There were very few rescue boats available and after the attack the survivors got to shore on their own. The U-boat launched its attack by firing at a coal boat. The torpedo missed and hit the wharf. The explosion shook the whole island and roused the population from their sleep. Special Constable Norm Noseworthy was on the telephone in his office when the explosion knocked him over and broke every window in the office. Pieces of the wharf landed two hundred feet away. Canadians on the island returned fire but their shooting was so bad they killed a cow at St. Phillip's and tore up cabbage and potato patches.

Of the forty-three crew members of the *Rose Castle*, twenty-eight were killed during the U-boat attack. Twelve of the PLM's fifty crew also died. The twelve French victims were waked side by side at the police station at Wabana. After the war, the French government arranged for all twelve bodies to be returned to their homes in France for burial.

There were five Newfoundlanders on the *Rose Castle*. They were J. Fillier, H. King, W. McLellan, F. Burt and C. Hardy. The bell of the *Rose Castle* was washed ashore and later recovered and placed on display at the Canadian Legion Club on Bell Island. A part of the torpedo which destroyed the wharf was recovered by a Canadian Corvette and taken to St. John's for examination.

The German captain was not just shooting in the dark that night. According to some Bell Island residents the captain had personally visited the island the day before the attack to assess its defences. He later sent a postcard to a Bell Island girl he had danced with the night before the attack.

THE RMS NEWFOUNDLAND

The Royal Mail Ship *Newfoundland* was owned by Furness Witty and Company and was well known throughout Newfoundland, initially as a troop carrier and later as a hospital ship. On September 2, 1943, the RMS *Newfoundland*, operating as a hospital ship and flying the Red Cross flag, was anchored with three other medical ships off Agropoli, Italy. There was heavy fighting on nearby Salerno Beach and the vessels were assigned to move in at intervals and remove the wounded from the beaches. At 11:00 a.m. German aircraft dropped a bomb which exploded between the *Newfoundland* and the *St. Andrew*. The attack missed the ships and there was no damage. The vessels were then moved to a less hazardous anchorage point.

The captain of the *Newfoundland*, J. E. Wilson, was puzzled by the attack. It was broad daylight and the vessels targeted were all hospital ships and all clearly flying the Red Cross flag. Wilson wondered if it had been deliberate. If so it was a contravention of the Geneva Convention. Any doubts held by the military were dispelled the next day when a deliberate dive-bombing assault was made on The *Newfoundland*, *St. Andrew*, *Leinster* and *Amara Poora* as they were preparing to re-enter the beaches to take the wounded on board. The *Newfoundland* was hit and instantly there was a fire. Several of the life boats were damaged. Rescue boats from other ships were used to evacuate the burning *Newfoundland*. The ship's fire fighting equipment had been destroyed in the strike and Wilson seeing the hopelessness of fighting the blaze ordered everyone to abandon ship.

My interest in this story stemmed from a picture postcard of the RMS *Newfoundland* sent to me by Mr. Bob Rumsey, a St. John's school teacher requesting some information on the sinking of the vessel. The card claimed it had been sunk by the German attack at Salerno. When researching the story, I found a letter Captain Wilson had written to the commander of the Mediterranean Fleet protesting the sinking of the

RMS *Newfoundland*. However, contrary to the post-card's claim, the vessel had not been sunk by German attack but rather by order of Allied forces. After the German attack, several American gun boats managed to put out the fire on the *Newfoundland*. Wilson inspected the damages and concluded the ship could be salvaged and repaired within twelve months. He requested a tug be sent to tow it to a nearby harbour for repairs. However, authorities decided that due to the situation on shore the tug could not be spared. Instead they ordered Allied ships to sink the RMS *Newfoundland*. Using seventy shells the RMS *Newfoundland* was sent to the ocean's bottom, causing Captain Wilson's protest to the Allied commander.

TRAGEDIES,
NATURAL DISASTERS
AND
HUMAN ERROR

A Fatal Wreck

When the 385 men, women and children passengers on the *Harpooner* set out for England from Quebec, they had no idea of the horror that awaited them off the Newfoundland coast. As the vessel neared St. Shott's on November 10, 1816, heavy winds and thick fog caused her to go off course and she struck rocks not far from Cape Freel's.

After sizing up the damage the captain realized the uselessness of the situation. He called all passengers and crewmen on deck intending to evacuate the ship. At this point his problems worsened. The lifeboats had been washed away by heavy seas and a burning candle had caused a fire in a cabin below deck.

The two stern boats still afloat were not nearly enough to rescue almost 400 people, so the captain decided to use them to send a lifeline to shore. That effort failed when the heavy seas forced the crew members making the attempt to take refuge on a small rocky island near the shore. Meanwhile, those still stranded on the sinking and burning vessel got some relief from their horror. A large wave came over the side and put the fire out. All on board were now on deck, some on hands and knees clinging to each other, others clinging to the sides and almost everyone praying. Just as everything seemed hopeless someone remembered the ship's dog and suggested that a rope be tied to him and he be sent ashore. In desperation the captain accepted the idea but decided to wait until dawn. At that time the rope was tied around the dog and his instincts seemed to tell him what to do for he swam straight for the men stranded on the rocks. The men then secured the line around a huge rock.

The captain hooked up a bosun's chair to ferry people from the ship and the rescue operations started. Many, however, perished on the deck of the ship while others, mostly women and children fell into the sea and drowned. At 11:00 a.m., with the rescue operation still in effect, the heaviest sea of all struck and smashed the ship into several pieces. Those still on deck awaiting rescue were swept into the sea. Men, women and children clinging to each other and screaming until only the sounds of the raging sea could be heard.

A rescue team from Trepassey arrived the following morning and removed to safety those who had managed to get to the rocks. The rescuers brought along some food and a little clothing, but after the survivors had eaten they went through several hours of hardship. They had to walk sixteen miles through woods to Trepassey with most of them still wet and cold. The famous Diver Dobbin was sent to the area weeks later and recovered the bodies and valuables from the *Harpooner* which then lay on the ocean's bottom. The wreck of the *Harpooner*, with 206 deaths, was the worst sea disaster in Newfoundland until the *Anglo-Saxon* disaster in 1863.

HUNGER, FROST AND CANNIBALISM STALKED THEM

The seventy-four men aboard the brigantine *Valliant* were not concerned about the shortage of lifeboats on board when they set sail from St. Malo, France for St. Pierre to take part in the fishery off Miquelon during April 1897. But five weeks later when they arrived on the Grand Banks some of them were ready to kill in order to gain a place on one of the nine, four-man dories being dispatched from the vessel after she struck an iceberg on the Banks. Twenty minutes later the *Valliant* was going to the bottom of the ocean and the screams of the dying men on board were terrifying to those who had managed to get into the dories.

The ordeal for the thirty-eight who went down with the ship ended in minutes but the suffering and ordeal of the survivors was just starting. They had to leave the ship so fast that they had no time to gather their clothing, blankets, provisions or even oars for the lifeboats. They now found themselves on the open sea with temperatures near freezing and a snowy spray surrounding them.

One boat carried seven men who worked so hard to bail out the incoming water which was drenching them to the skin, that they quickly became feeble and exhausted. Their gnawing pangs of hunger increased by the hour. Two men died and were thrown over-board to make room for the others.

When the third man passed away the famishing survivors cut some strips of flesh from the corpse and began eating it. When they were rescued only half the body was left. The survivors were covered in masses of white gangrened frostbitten flesh. They were so badly frostbitten that each of them had to have various limbs amputated. Only three survived the operations that followed. They lost legs, arms, ears and noses.

A second lifeboat was rescued a day later. The suffering on the boat was terrible. However, they had not resorted to cannibalism as their friends had done. Instead when hunger began driving them insane, they killed the ship's dog and ate that. The frozen spray that constantly battered them had encased the men in ice-solid clothes. The hunger and cold caused several on board to act erratically and the others had to restrain them from turning the lifeboat over.

When rescuers found them they were all near unconsciousness lying on the bottom of the boat, and had given up all hope of being found.

A Story of Heroism

Neither the freezing Atlantic waters nor sixty-four hours of exposure to winter temperatures were enough to defeat George Piercey of Green Island, Fortune Bay. Piercey overcame all these hardships and in the process saved a man's life and earned himself a Royal Humane Society medal for heroism.

Piercey was cook on the thirty-ton schooner *B.C. McGrath* when it set out on a return trip to Fortune from St. Pierre. About a half mile from Pass Island the ship ran into a blinding snowstorm and waves carried away its rudder. Within fifty yards of the mainland, the ship grounded on a small rock. Captain Alford, realizing there were no life boats on board, ordered his two crew members to jump to a rock about four feet away. The heavy blowing snow made it impossible at times to see or judge the distance of the rock from the ship. All three men succeeded in jumping to the rock, but were up to their waists in water as the sea swept over it, making it impossible for them to keep their footing. The skipper was ready to give up. The ship's mate John Woodland couldn't swim and Piercey was not a strong swimmer. When Alford suggested they would have a chance if they could secure a line, Piercey made the treacherous jump back to the sinking vessel. He picked up a line and jumped back to the rock. Although cold and frightened, Piercey tied the rope around himself while his friends held the other end. He them jumped into the raging seas and fought his way to shore. Piercey pulled Woodland to safety. He then tied one end of the rope to a rock, the other end around himself and went back into the water to rescue the Captain. After getting Alford safely to shore, Piercey led them up a perpendicular cliff which was covered with ice and snow. For hours they walked knee deep in snow and then a glimpse of hope appeared. In the distance they saw a small hut. But again fate played a cruel trick on them.

The hut turned out to be an ice house, but at least it protected them from the harsh winter winds. Woodland died of exposure. Piercey dragged the Captain through miles of blinding snow until they found safety at Grole. Piercey and Alford were home in time to spend Christmas with their families.

On May 8, 1936, Piercey was awarded the Royal Humane Society's Bronze Medal and a certificate for bravery in recognition of his heroic deeds.

INDIAN-MEAL WINTER

The year 1868 is remembered in Newfoundland history as the Winter of the Indian Meal. The bottom had fallen out of the Newfoundland economy. Fishermen couldn't sell their catch and their boats were repossessed by creditors. The advent of winter added to the hardship. People were dying of hunger all over the Island. Farm animals were also dropping dead from hunger and the population reverted to looting houses and cellars in search of anything edible. To assist the starving population the government doled out Indian meal which consisted of yellow corn and molasses. No other food was given and consequently the name Indian-Meal Winter.

Temperatures plummeted to the lowest in twenty-five years and people dropped dead in the streets and fields from hunger and exposure. Exhausted by hunger, men and women would fall into the snow and freeze to death. It was one of the worst years in all Newfoundland history.

EARTHQUAKE &
TIDAL WAVE

A fault in the earth located 250 miles south of St. John's on the extreme northern end of the Grand Banks, was once the epicentre of a great earthquake that was felt throughout the Maritimes and the New England states, causing a devastating tidal wave along Newfoundland's southwest coast. The earthquake which registered 7.2 on the Richter scale caused harbours from St. Lawrence to Lamaline to drain dry and later refill with a fifty foot tidal wave that brought death and destruction.

When the earthquake first struck, a loud blasting sound was heard in St. John's. Most people thought it was an explosion at the Bell Island mines. Transatlantic cables were damaged, and it was not until four days later that the outside world became aware of the devastation that followed it. The event represented the first reported earthquake that far east from the main seismic belts. Scientists considered it, at a magnitude of 7.2, to be major in terms of energy release.

The earthquake occurred on a fine day, November 18, 1929, around 4:30 p.m., it lasted a few minutes, then stopped. One eyewitness reported that the road near Lamaline appeared as if it were moving. Buckets of water looked as though they were boiling. In stores, goods fell off the shelves and houses shook. Nobody knew what had happened and it was the talk of the town at suppertime that night. A resident later reported, "At eight o'clock a woman rushed into my store and shouted that all the water was gone out of the harbour. We went out to see. It seemed as though the end of the world was at hand. The harbour was dry and all the boats and schooners were on their sides. People ran from the town and by the time I cleared up, got my family and started to leave, there was nobody left here. The town was silent and then I heard the start of a roar, it got louder and louder. Fortunately everyone was heading for high ground. Then we saw this great tidal wave rushing in and rooting up homes and buildings."

Later when rescuers tried to recover property floating in the bay and to look for survivors and bodies, they found a house with a child upstairs in its cot still asleep while the rest of the family on the first floor had all drowned. Twenty-nine people lost their lives before the tidal wave subsided. The search for bodies went on until the following autumn. The tidal wave lasted about two hours and caused two million dollars worth of damage to the southwest coast. All marine growth was swept away and the fish did not return to the area until the 1940s.

On November 25 a south coast disaster committee was set up in St. John's with the governor as chairman.

The group raised a quarter of a million dollars to help those affected by the disaster. Financial assistance also came from all over the world to aid the victims.

THE BIGGEST HOLLYWOOD DISASTER

Many readers will be surprised to learn that the biggest Hollywood movie disaster was not the one in South Asia which claimed the life of movie star Victor Morrow . . . but the *Viking* disaster which occurred in Newfoundland on March 12, 1931.

Producer Varrick Frizell had already filmed the movie *White Thunder* which dealt with the seal hunt off Newfoundland's coast. However the brass at Paramount felt the picture needed more action to liven it up and consequently Frizell planned to return to the ice and film an iceberg tipping over. To create this action scene he planned to use dynamite, which had been placed on board by the Paramount movie crew.

On the evening of the tragedy Frizell and his friends were discussing a book entitled *Vikings of the North* which dealt with the dangers faced by men at sea. As the men discussed the book Frizell noted to the others that the dynamite they had brought on board was poorly stored in the hallways. At the suggestion of one of the crew Frizell took it upon himself to make a sign which read Danger–Explosives. He intended hanging it outside a storage room in the hall which housed the bulk of the dynamite. He never finished the sign. Midway through, the ship exploded. Frizell was blown right out of the ship and never heard from again. The explosion caused the death of thirty-three men, including all but one of the Hollywood crew.

One of the heroes of that tragedy was Pat (Louis) Breen of Flower Hill, St. John's. Breen led a band of six men back on board the burning ship. With flames shooting high into the air and the *Viking* still being rocked by explosions, Breen systematically gathered supplies and provisions to help the surviving crew who were then stranded on the ice. Breen gathered food, burlap to wrap the injured and cut off the dories which were used to carry the wounded to safety.

Breen and his men got off the ship without any injuries then helped place the injured in the dories. They tied rope to the dories and organized groups of men to drag them over ten miles of broken ice until they reached the safety of Horse Islands.

Breen's feet became frostbitten and he later had his toes amputated. Friends of Breen say he was never recognized for his deeds and rarely spoke about the disaster.

THE DEATH OF DR. BANTING

On the evening of February 21, 1941, a Lockheed Hudson, similar to the one on display near Gander airport, set out from Gander for England carrying a world famous doctor and scientist. A short while later the plane crashed near Musgrave Harbour and only one of the four men on board survived. Sir Frederick Banting, co-discoverer of insulin — considered one of the world's greatest medical advances — was one of the victims. News of the tragedy made international headlines.

At fifty, Banting had had a most distinguished

career. In 1923 he was awarded the Nobel Prize for physiology and medicine in recognition of his part in the discovery of insulin. Ten years later he was made a Knight of the British Empire. At the time of his death during World War II, Banting was travelling on a special mission to England in connection with the Empire Air Training Program.

The aircraft pilot was Captain Joe Mackey of Kansas City, a civilian pilot who made a living flying planes across the Atlantic. When search planes discovered the location of the crashed plane they dropped leaflets over the Musgrave Harbour area telling the people where it was and that there appeared to be a survivor. When rescuers arrived at the scene Mackey was in a sleeping bag, his head bandaged but still alive. The navigator was lying dead near the plane's doorway, the co-pilot, still strapped to his seat, was also killed in the crash. Banting survived long enough to bandage Mackey's head and place him in a sleeping bag. The doctor then wandered from the crash site and perished. Sam Harris of Carnell's Funeral Services in St. John's was flown to Gander to prepare Banting's body for burial, which took place at Toronto.

Probably because it was wartime, the prevailing rumour was that the plane had been sabotaged. It was widely believed that saboteurs had put sand in the plane's oil supply causing the engine to falter.

The Canadian government appointed Air Commodore G. V. Walsh to investigate these allegations, however he found no grounds to substantiate them. Captain Mackey, twenty years after the incident, continued to hold fast to his belief that the plane had been sabotaged.

The World's Greatest Mass Collision of Ships

During 1942 a large convoy of seventy-six westbound Allied vessels was making its way steadily through a dense fog in Newfoundland waters. One ship struck an iceberg around the same time that eight other icebergs were sighted nearby. A general alarm was sounded to warn others in the convoy of the impending danger. Instantly, all vessels in the vicinity turned sharply to avoid hitting the icebergs and the result was the biggest collision of ships in history. Twenty-two vessels collided and one went to the bottom of the Atlantic. Fortunately, there was no loss of life in spite of the great confusion and damage. The convoy continued on its mission and the event was classified as top secret.

Oops! There Goes Our Dactyle!

The archaeological find of the twentieth century was made on Bell Island around the turn of the century. Lack of knowledge of its value resulted in its destruction and loss to history. Workmen stripping number two mine on the island uncovered something in the cave's wall that puzzled them. They called in Frank Kneeland a consulting engineer with Dosco who held a bachelor of science degree. It didn't take long for Kneeland to determine the find as a fossil containing the remains of the extinct species pterodactyl, a winged reptile.

The reptile measured over twenty feet between wing tips. It showed a long neck, the head was missing, the body elongated with a long tail but its claws were not visible. Aware of the great historical value of this find, Kneeland decided to package it and send it off to the famous Institute in Washington. He carefully arranged to have every speck of dust cleaned off, and made sure no one meddled with it. He then patiently made a drawing of the dactyl and proceeded to remove it in pieces from the walls of shale rock. As he removed the pieces he carefully numbered them to easily facilitate their reassembly.

Kneeland then ordered two employees from Bell Island to take the material by horse and cart to the draughting office of Dosco. Leaving the men to carry out their task Kneeland returned to his office to supervise the construction of specially prepared boxes to be used to transport the find to the Smithsonian Institute. The workers meanwhile had no idea of the value of their cargo as Kneeland neglected to explain it to them.

After arriving in front of Kneeland's office, instead of removing the fossil piece by piece they literally dumped the whole cargo onto the ground, smashing it into tens of thousands of pieces. Kneeland was horrified by their action.

A newspaper reference to the costly error at Bell Island noted, "Not all the King's horses, nor all the King's men could put that reptile together again."

POLITICS
AND
RELIGION

Execution on Belvedere Street

The political situation in Newfoundland during the year 1800 was explosive. Fanned by reports that the British had suffered a number of defeats in Europe and the abolition of the Irish Parliament, a group of Irish military men at Fort William developed a plan to take control of the fort and the City of St. John's.

The conspirators planned to lead an uprising during Sunday Mass on April 20, then proceed to the Church of England to take all the officers and the leading inhabitants prisoners. Roman Catholic Archbishop J. Louis O'Donnell, an Irishman himself, had little sympathy for the Irish rebels and felt their violent activities back in Ireland were a disgrace to the Catholic church. O'Donnell learned of the plot and advised Brigadier General Skerrett, the commanding officer at the Fort. When Sunday arrived the general foiled rebel plans by sending them on manoeuvres instead of on the usual church parade.

The action only delayed the rebels' plans and on the night of April 24 about twenty of them deserted their regiments and assembled at a powder shed on the barrens. Others from the fort were prevented from joining them after an alarm had been raised at the fort. Two days later, the rebels were confronted by loyalist troops in the woods near St. John's. Most of them escaped, however eight were captured and tried for treason. After being sentenced to death, the men were taken to the site where they planned their crime and hanged. (A plaque marks the place on Belvedere Street where the executions took place.) Following their execution the eight men were left hanging in chains as a spectacle and deterrent for others who might consider rebellion.[2]

There was strong support for the rebels among the people of St. John's who were mostly Irish. United Irish support was sparked around the island and Skerrett had to reinforce the garrison at Placentia. The Irish supporters were controlled by a directorate of five men. O'Donnell's part in foiling the uprising is disputed by historians, however they acknowledged the strong possibility that he did play a major role in calming the civilian population and preventing any support for the rebels from townspeople.

[2]   Historical records over the centuries vary on the number executed and the place of execution. Since the sentence included gibbeting, it is likely that after the executions the gibbeting took place on Signal Hill. Gibbeting, whereby the executed person would be left on public display, was meant to be a deterrent. The powder shed behind Fort Townshend in the area now known as Belvedere Street would not have served this purpose. While some records refer to the men being hanged on Signal Hill and left on the gibbet; the gibbet there had been removed in 1795 to make way for Wallace Battery. It is possible that after the executions at the powder shed, a gibbet was constructed on Signal Hill to display the rebels. Yet, there are some claims that the men were taken to Halifax, paraded through the streets and publicly executed there.

THE BISHOP AND THE KING

King William IV of England had a close connection with Newfoundland. While the king was still a prince he spent a great deal of time in this province. William was a down-to-earth person and made many close friends among the inhabitants of St. John's and in Bay Bulls where he served a term as surrogate magistrate. The prince came to the aid of a fisherman named O'Driscoll by representing him in court. O'Driscoll, thanks to Prince William's efforts, became the first Newfoundland fisherman to recover money from a merchant.

Another example of the prince's common touch took place near Quidi Vidi. A Mr. Warren was walking home one night carrying a lantern to guide his way. Suddenly the lantern was snatched from his hand by a man who wished him good night and offered to walk along with him through the foggy dark night until he was safely home. At Warren's home the man passed the lantern back to him and departed. It was Prince William.

A local woman presented the prince with a gift of a wild goose and the prince responded by promoting her husband who became a lieutenant in the Royal Navy. However there was another side to Prince William . . . he was a religious bigot holding strong dislike for Roman Catholics. In 1786 he wrote Governor Elliott complaining about the deplorable influence of Father Burke in Placentia.

The Roman Catholic Bishop O'Donnell complained to the governor about the prince's efforts to hinder development of the Church in Newfoundland. The governor relayed the complaint to the king.

Thereafter, whenever the prince met the bishop he would openly insult him and on one occasion he tossed an iron file through the palace window which struck O'Donnell, almost breaking his shoulder. Prince William's harassment of Bishop O'Donnell continued and the bishop learned that the prince was planning to kill him and claim he was responding to an insult from the bishop. In addition, the prince planned to burn down the Roman Catholic church on Henry Street.

O'Donnell hid out in the attic of a friend's home for more than two weeks. Not even the friend's family was aware that the bishop was in the house. When the prince left Newfoundland, O'Donnell came out of hiding. The bishop kept quiet about the incident to avoid adding to religious strife in Newfoundland and Ireland.

Expelled by the Vatican

For several years before the Orange Riot in Harbour Grace, which claimed five lives, there was more fighting among factions within the community's Roman Catholic church than between Catholics and Protestants. One such dispute was between the bishop and his faction and the BIS (Benevolent Irish Society) and its supporters and was only resolved after intercession from the Vatican.

The trouble started when Bishop Carfagnini and his secretary Diomedes Falconio condemned the BIS for having accepted Protestants into its membership. Falconio argued that the bishop held absolute authority over the BIS while the BIS argued it was a civil and mixed society. Falconio's position divided Catholics throughout the Harbour Grace and Carbonear area. The Italian priest denounced all who opposed the bishop and encouraged others to shun them because they were wicked in the eyes of God. This was an opinion not shared by other Catholic clergymen throughout the Island.

While Falconio was stirring up dissent, his superior Bishop Carfagnini was attempting to develop good relations with non-Catholic churches in the area. Carfagnini was actually popular among Protestants. When Head Constable Fallon of Harbour Grace, a member of the BIS, passed away, his wife requested the bishop to permit her husband to be buried with a requiem mass. The bishop decreed that Fallon would only be buried with a requiem mass if the BIS members removed their scarves and shoulder sashes. Meanwhile, the bishop's supporters organized the Conception Bay BIS. The original BIS had support from priests at St. John's and Falconio attacked them as well. He warned that any Catholic attending the BIS funeral would be excommunicated. He reasoned that the BIS would not be allowed inside the church because there were Protestants among its member ship. This was not consistent, in view of the fact that a few days before, the sister of a priest was buried with a requiem high mass which was attended by all the leading Freemasons and Orangemen. Also, when prominent merchant Robert Munn died, several of the bishop's supporters went to the Presbyterian church. The dispute caused a serious drop in church attendance.

Roman Catholic priests in St. John's petitioned the Vatican to remove the bishop, which resolved the situation. Carfagnini was transferred to Gallipoli, Italy, as an archbishop. Falconio, years later became a cardinal, and the Conception Bay Benevolent Irish Society was abandoned.

THE ORANGE RIOTS

The surfacing of religious bigotry at Harbour Grace during 1883 resulted in five shooting deaths and seventeen other people being wounded. William French of Courage's Beach was shot twice in the head and had sixty-two wounds on the front of his body. Moses Nicholas of Mayne's Brook had twenty-six shots in him. The Orange Riot, as it is known in Harbour Grace history, resulted when Orangemen clashed with Riverhead Catholics near Pippy's Lane. For several years prior to the riot of July 12, 1883, the Orange Parade had been hampered by sporadic trouble and police had to be called in several times. On the day of this tragic confrontation the Catholic population feared that the Orangemen intended on marching into their community to cause trouble.

Determined to stop this from happening, the Riverhead men gathered near Pippy's Lane, the boundary at that time, and requested Constable Edward Doyle to order the parade to take another route. It is unlikely that the Orangemen planned on marching into Riverhead but they refused police requests and went on to Pippy's Lane. Many of the Riverhead men were armed, as were many of the spectators. However there was no evidence of the Orangemen themselves being armed. What happened when the groups confronted each other at Pippy's Lane remains a mystery. Accusations were made that Constable Doyle fired the first shot causing the death of Patrick Callahan.

This was certainly untrue, because the bullet retrieved from Callahan's body weighed twenty-two grams while the bullet of Doyle's gun weighed eighty-two grams. While the cause of the riot has never been determined, one thing was certain and that was the Orangemen got the worst of it. Four of the five murder victims were members of the Loyal Orange Association and twelve of the seventeen wounded were Orangemen or their supporters. Twenty-six men including Head Constable Edward Doyle were arrested following that incident.

THE IRA DEATH SQUAD VISIT

An IRA death squad once visited St. John's. Their target . . . a city resident who at one time was commander of the famous Black and Tans, a para-military organization sent by British Prime Minister Lloyd George to put down civil unrest in Ireland during the early 1920s.

Sir Hugh Tudor had a lot of military experience and was a lifetime friend of another British Prime Minister, Sir Winston Churchill. When Tudor was wounded during the Boer War and hospitalized, Churchill sent him a wire saying, "Best wishes for a happy Christmas, swift recovery and all the luck of the war." During the First World War, Tudor was commander of the Ninth Scottish Division in France and he is recognized in history as the inventor of the smoke screen used in later warfare.

The Black and Tans was made up of unemployed ex-British soldiers serving as auxiliary members of the Royal Irish Constabulary. When Tudor's unit was formed, there were not enough uniforms to go around and consequently the forces combined parts of the army uniform with parts of the Royal Irish Constabulary uniform. Seeing this mixture of khaki and black, the Irish quickly dubbed the military force as the Black and Tans, a name referring to a famous pack of Irish hounds. While in Ireland, Tudor was also head of the Royal Irish Constabulary and the Dublin Metropolitan Police Force.

Liam Deasey, a commander of the IRA at that time, later said that Tudor had backed all the excesses of the Black and Tans.

When Sir Hugh Tudor retired from service he sought out a place where the IRA wouldn't find him. He moved to Bonavista and left his wife and two sons in England for he felt they would be safer with him out of the country.

The IRA however, tracked him down. Tudor had moved from Bonavista to St. John's. The death squad came to the city and spent a few weeks preparing their assassination plan. This was their first assignment to kill and they sought the advice of a Catholic priest at the Basilica. Upon hearing their story, the priest ordered them to leave the country within twenty-four hours or he would report them to local authorities. The squad heeded his warning and the IRA never bothered Sir Hugh again. On September 25, 1965, blind and at the age of ninety-five, Sir Hugh Tudor passed away. It was ironic that Tudor who held a life-long hatred for the Irish spent his latter years being cared for by an Irish-Newfoundland housekeeper, Monica McCarthy.

POLITICAL INGENUITY

During the period Sir Edward Morris served as prime minister of Newfoundland, from 1909–1918, Roman Catholics strictly adhered to their church's rule of abstinence from eating meat on Fridays. Sir Edward Morris once found himself in political hot water when word had reached his enemies in St. John's that he had eaten meat on a Friday during a visit to a Protestant community at Grand Bank.

In those days such a violation of church rules by a public figure would be enough to ruin him politically. Sir Edward's enemies in Kilbride hoped to turn the Catholic vote in St. John's West against the prime minister. On his return from Grand Bank he was scheduled to speak at a rally in Kilbride. His enemies packed the hall. Their leaders were planning on raising the issue and confronting Sir Edward Morris in the presence of his loyal supporters.

Anticipating this sort of trouble, the politically shrewd Morris rose before the meeting started, to make a few remarks. He began by denouncing the vile rumours circulating that he had sacrificed his religion by eating meat on Friday to get votes in a Protestant district. Morris told the crowd that he did eat meat at Grand Bank, but that in fact he was in a delicate state of health with problems similar to that of the archbishop. He then plucked a document from his pocket which in reality was a life insurance policy and began reading improvised Latin phrases. Holding the deed up for the crowd to see, he claimed it was a papal document of dispensation from the Vatican.

He concluded with a denunciation of his opponents for criticizing the pope's authority. Completely won over, his enemies surged toward the stage, lifted Morris on their shoulders and carried him around the Kilbride hall in a victory procession.

RARE AND REMARKABLE NEWFOUNDLANDERS

THE MAD PROPHET

The Mad Prophet of Placentia, was a man once taken seriously by thousands of people in Europe. Richard Brothers was the founder of a religious sect that put forward the theory that the Anglo Saxon race is one of the lost tribes of Israel. Brothers, who was born at Admiral's Beach, Fermeuse on December 25, 1757, and spent part of his life at Placentia, anointed himself as the apostle of a new religion, the nephew of the Almighty and the prince of the Hebrews. He claimed to have been chosen to lead the Hebrews to the land of Canaan. Two years later he released his book, *A Revealed Knowledge of the Prophets and Times*.

Brothers developed a following throughout Britain and the United States after correctly forecasting the death of King Gustav III of Sweden and the guillotine death of King Louis XVI of France. Prominent wealthy people consulted with him regularly and it was a common sight to see a traffic jam of coaches outside his London home. One of his strongest supporters was a wealthy London lawyer, John Finlayson. On one occasion he wrote to the king, the prime minister and the speaker of the House of Commons advising them he had divine instructions to present himself at the Bar of the House. There was no reply to his letter and at the appointed time he presented himself at the Commons. The speaker ordered him to leave. He then sent a letter to the king and queen which upset the king very much.

He claimed that we was the rightful king of England and intended to claim the throne. The letter was published along with his prophesy that the world would be destroyed by fire on August 15, 1793, but his efforts with the Almighty would cause London to be saved.

King George III ordered that Brothers be brought before the privy council and charged with treason. He was declared insane and confined to a mental asylum at Islington. His supporters, led by the influential Finlayson, fought for eleven years to have him released. British M.P. Nathaniel Halhed, the first man to set up a printing press in India, also used his money and power to help Brothers during this period. In 1806 the charge of treason was dropped and the Mad Prophet was released into the custody of Finlayson with whom he lived until his death on January 25, 1824. His last words to his friend was a request that his religion be carried on. Edward Hinse became the leader at that time and he continued the Mad Prophet's religion until 1891 when he too passed away.

THE ECCENTRIC DANIELLE

During the latter part of the nineteenth century one of the most colourful and eccentric characters in all Newfoundland was Professor Charles Henry Danielle. Danielle is best remembered as the owner, builder and operator of the famous Octagon Castle on Topsail Road. Danielle built the castle to use as a hotel and hoped to attract honeymooners to his lavishly deco-rated bridal suite. The room had been adorned with satin, lace and plush, in silver and gold colours. Danielle even designed a special quilt for the bridal chamber. It took him two years to make it using eighty-five yards of material at a cost of eight hundred dol-lars, a princely sum in those days.

All his efforts failed to lure newlyweds and the disheartened Danielle commented, "It broke my heart that my suite of rooms is no longer on the market as a resort for newlyweds. I am going to rear a couple of pigs in the bridal suite. It will pay me better."

On another occasion when customers complained that the milk at the castle had been watered down, Danielle defended himself, claiming in a newspaper letter that rain must have seeped somewhere into the cows. To remedy this he built a number of shingled roofs and attached them to the backs of his cows.

Another oddity of Danielle, was the room at the castle displaying his glass-lidded casket. The casket was covered in black satin embroidered with gold and the interior upholstery was made with eight thousand white satin shells. It included a white satin pillow, white satin shroud and golden slippers.

Prior to opening the castle, Danielle had operated lavish restaurants at Quidi Vidi Lake and Water Street. He also operated a dance school and hosted many costume balls in the city.

Danielle had originally come as a visitor to Newfoundland from Baltimore, Maryland. He fell in love with his host country and decided to make it his home. In May 1902 he died and his funeral attracted crowds of curious people. He was laid to rest in a marble vault at the Anglican Cemetery on Forest Road.

DIVER DOBBIN

Diver Dobbin was a remarkable Newfoundlander. He pioneered the use of diving suits in Newfoundland — and perhaps Canada — and was the same man who sent shock waves around the world by discovering the bodies of seventy-three murder victims in the cabins of a sunken ship near Burin. Dobbin spent fourteen years using the diving suit to salvage sunken ships and locate treasures of all kinds around Newfoundland and Labrador. During that period he overhauled fifty-one vessels of various tonnages, from a fishing schooner to an Atlantic liner. His share of the discoveries was $25,000 over expenses, an amount considered a fortune in those days.

A tin, a half pint measure made by tinsmiths in St. John's and used for drinking tea on the fishing ground and by poor families at home, was called a 'Dobbin' in honour of our diving hero. Newfoundland historian, P. K. Devine once described him saying, "This man of indomitable courage had experiences unique and terrifying, that would put modern novelists in the imagining for thrills and kicks; in the shade."

Without any previous experience or coaching, he donned a diving suit and dropped down into the cold and unknown depths of the sea. He calmly handled and attached to tackles many mangled bodies of human beings as if they were merely bags of bread and barrels of flour. Dobbin was called in to salvage valuables from the sunken schooner *Harpooner* which went down on November 10, 1816, near Cape Pine. That was the most serious wreck on the Newfoundland coast up to that time, since more people died as a result than from any previous wreck. There were 385 men, women and children on board. Most of the men were from the Fourth Royal Veteran Battalion. Dobbin worked on the *Harpooner* until all the copper and moveable parts were recovered from the ship.

A vessel known as a free booter, that worked the

Spanish Main in pirate raids in winter and the Newfoundland coast during the summer months, was lost in Baccalieu Tickle near Red Head Cove. Smith McKay, a wealthy developer in Newfoundland at the time, investigated the story and discovered that a Mr. Avery of Red Head Cove had recovered two kegs of the gold from the bottom.

McKay hired the schooner *Snake* and enlisted the services of Diver Dobbin. Dobbin spent several days in the area but found no trace of the sunken ship or treasure. Or so he reported. Dobbin had many adventures along Newfoundland coasts. Although a fortune passed through his hands in his lifetime, he spent freely and lavishly and at the time of his death in 1893, his savings had been almost wiped out.

A Renowned Newfoundland Shipbuilder

Daniel Condon, born at Aquaforte in 1840, helped put Newfoundland in the history books by his great achievements as a shipbuilder, which made him famous all over the world. In 1877 Condon's skill as a shipbuilder was already widely acclaimed throughout Newfoundland. That same year, the *Captain Steward*, a ship owned by the New England Lines Company, on her maiden voyage from Liverpool to Boston, was grounded on Great Island, around twenty-five miles from St. John's, after being lost in a dense fog.

Lloyd's of London, who stood to lose a large sum of money if the ship was written off, sent their ablest ship expert, Captain Chisholm, to try and refloat the stranded vessel. For thirty days Chisholm attempted by every means he knew to refloat the ship but all efforts failed. During this period numerous people mentioned bringing in Dan Condon. Chisholm, in desperation, consulted with Condon and when Condon presented him with a plan to refloat the *Captain Steward*, Chisholm was amused. Condon had invented the world's first pontoons and when Chisholm viewed them he laughed and referred to them as 'match boxes.'

Nevertheless, Condon used his new invention and succeeded in refloating the ship. Word of Condon's invention spread — as did the use of pontoons — all over the world. Condon's reputation grew even more after he invented the cofferdam, a miniature dry dock. When the world's largest ship at that time, the *Arizona*, experienced serious damage to her bow, she crippled into St. John's harbour to seek repairs. This was prior to the building of the drydock. Condon was consulted, and the *Arizona*'s experts were not impressed by his suggestion to replace the damaged bow with a wood and concrete one. However, the owner of the ship was on board and in desperation so he gave permission for Condon to proceed. Condon's idea worked. The owner was so delighted he gave Condon a five hundred pound bonus and a valuable painting from the ship. In addition he offered him a cruise on the *Arizona* to either Europe or Alaska. Condon politely refused.

Condon's inventions saved many ships. He was able to refloat several already sunken ships at Twillingate and Fogo. Word of the shipbuilding genius of Newfoundland spread and when the *Arizona* docked at Liverpool, thousands of curious people came from all parts of England to see his work. Sir Ambrose Shea was so impressed by Condon's ability that he commissioned him to build the first steamer ever constructed in Newfoundland, the *Isabella*.

Condon passed away on April 25, 1889 at the age of forty-nine.

Pomiuk-Angel of Peace

A little Eskimo boy named Pomiuk had a dramatic affect on the great humanitarian work of the famous Sir Wilfred Grenfell in northern Newfoundland and Labrador. Pomiuk was among fifty Labrador Eskimos chosen by American promoters to inhabit an Eskimo village at the Chicago World's Fair of 1892. Pomiuk's expertise and competence with the long whip drew many visitors to the exhibition.

Meanwhile, W. H. Whitley, a wealthy Newfoundland fisherman and inventor of the codtrap, teamed up with an old friend in New England and set out to visit the World's Fair. The old friend was Reverend C. C. Carpenter, a former missionary to Labrador and by then editor of the *Congregationalist*, a popular newspaper in the New England states. In addition to his duties as editor, Carpenter wrote a regular children's column using the name Mr. Martin. At the World's Fair, the two visitors sought out the Eskimo village and quickly made friends with the Eskimo population. When leaving, Carpenter gave Pomiuk a picture of himself and autographed it, Mr. Martin. Pomiuk placed the picture in a small bag that hung around his neck.

Just before returning to Newfoundland, the boy's stepfather beat him and inflicted a serious wound to the boy's leg which became infected. Back in

Labrador, the stepfather deserted Pomiuk who was then taken in by another family. On one of his medical journeys, Dr. Grenfell was told of a dying boy by the manager of the Hudson's Bay Company. Grenfell went and brought the boy to the manager's home and treated his infected leg. As he administered chloroform to Pomiuk, he removed the bag from his neck and noticed the picture. When Pomiuk recovered, he told Grenfell that the picture was of his friend Mr. Martin. Sometime later, in St. John's, Grenfell met Whitley and told him the story of the boy with the picture of Mr. Martin. Whitley explained who Mr. Martin was and advised Grenfell to visit him on his next trip to the United States.

Eventually, Grenfell set out for the U.S. to seek support for his missionary work in Labrador. The first person he sought out was Pomiuk's friend Mr. Martin. Grenfell was overwhelmed by the tremendous help and support given to him by Carpenter. Through his newspaper column, he told the story of Pomiuk and he invited children to send ten cents each to Grenfell to help provide medical services to the Eskimos. Donations poured in from everywhere and Carpenter then arranged a speaking tour for Grenfell which brought even more support. The final result was that Grenfell fulfilled his lifelong ambition. He got the money for the hospital and top U.S. doctors volunteered their services during the summer months to help Grenfell in treating the sick of northern Newfoundland. All this was made possible by Grenfell having the chance of meeting little Pomiuk. During the fall of 1897, little Pomiuk passed away as a result of the injuries inflicted on him by his stepfather. On his deathbed, he was christened with the name of Gabriel, meaning the angel of comfort.

World Known Event

Peter Edstrom, a well-known plumber in St. John's at the turn of the century, played an important role in a world-famous historical event that took place in Newfoundland on December 12, 1901. Just three weeks earlier, a ship had set out from England heading for St. John's. The ship's mission was to report that at a certain hour on December 12, a message would be sent from Ireland by wireless to America.

Meanwhile on Signal Hill at St. John's, five hundred feet above the oldest settlement in all North America, Marconi was feverishly working to set up his apparatus to receive the first transatlantic wireless message from the Old World. However, in order for Marconi to complete his work he required the services of a plumber to fuse together the wires which were the lifeline of the newly invented machinery.

Fusing together the wires seemed an impossibility to onlookers at Signal Hill because the wires were located at the bottom of a seventy-five-foot well. Edstrom was not deterred. He descended into the well with Marconi watching and knowing the success of his project depended on him. Edstrom ran into some difficulty and the project was delayed by three hours. When the apparatus was ready, world history was made as Marconi received the first wireless message from across the Atlantic.

Peter Edstrom later recalled that when he was training as a plumber, he earned fifty cents a week. After he completed his training, his salary doubled to one dollar weekly. He worked ten hours a day, with no holidays and only Sundays off. To put this into perspective, rum was eighty cents a bottle.

TOP SECRET

The Manhattan Project, a project that developed the world's first atomic bomb, was so well guarded that Vice-president, Harry S Truman, was not aware of its existence until he became president on the day of President F. D. Roosevelt's death in 1945. The project brought the world even closer to the brink of destruction. Its first explosion also set off the cold war between the East and the West.

When the bomb was being planned and developed, scientists from several allied countries were involved. Ten of these were Canadians and one of them was Ronald B. Winsor of Greenspond, Bonavista Bay. Winsor was involved in the project in his capacity as special assistant to the manager of Defence Industries Ltd.., special projects department. He was born in 1904, the son of Captain and Mrs. William Winsor of Bonavista Bay.

Defence Industries was responsible for the construction of a government-owned plant at Clarke River, Ontario which handled Canada's share of the development and production of atomic energy. Winsor was one of the select group throughout the Western world who had knowledge of and worked on the world's first atomic bomb.

SIR ROBERT REID

During the early 1940s, Sir Robert Reid of St. John's made Ripley's *Believe It Or Not*. His record was established for being the single largest landowner in all North America. This was made possible through a grant to Reid by the Newfoundland government which gave him over five million acres of land as well as most of the ore, minerals, docks, telegraph lines, steamships and railroad in Newfoundland. Under that contract a railway was to be constructed from St. John's to Port aux Basques within three years. This was to be paid for by the grant of land which amounted to ·five thousand acres for each mile constructed plus other valuable considerations.

World Famous Artist

At the turn of the century the toast of the Parisian art world and the gentle artistic genius whose paintings fetched the highest price ever paid up to that time to a Canadian painter was Maurice Cullen. Cullen was born at Harbour Grace on June 6, 1866, and is credited with introducing impressionism to Canada.

Journalist Barbara MacAndrews writing in the *Atlantic Advocate* stated, "He changed the perspective of traditional art in this country by creating impressions through images seen in his own eyes." An exhibition of seventy of Cullen's finest works have travelled to art galleries all across Canada.

Cullen left school at an early age and went to work in a drygoods store. He showed an interest in sculpture and eventually moved to Paris on the advice of Canadian sculptor Phillipe Hebert. Cullen spent long hours copying the great masters and switched from sculpture to painting. He enrolled in advanced art classes. Once his work went on display he became an instant hit throughout the French art world. One of his first paintings, a snowy scene in Brittany was purchased by the French government., which also purchased other Cullen paintings. Maurice Cullen became the first Canadian to be made a member of the Societé National des Beaux Arts in Paris.

Maurice Cullen, tired of the Parisian art world, moved to Montreal to settle down and continue his work. In 1907 he was made a full member of the Royal Academy of Art. He became employed as an art teacher for the Catholic School Commission of Montreal. Cullen was then commissioned by the Canadian government to do paintings of the government war cemeteries in France. He had four stepsons one of whom was killed during World War I.

Newfoundland's Maurice Cullen played an important role in Canada's artistic development. His oil and pastel works were very popular and he received the largest amount of money ever paid to a Canadian artist, up to that time frame, at a single show. That was $8,775 for a painting sold in 1928, an amount undreamed of by artists during that period.

When Cullen passed away on March 28, 1934, S. Morgan Powell, art critic for the *Montreal Star* wrote, "Canadian art loses one of its most eminent exponents, and Canada an artist of the first rank, through the death of Maurice Cullen. As an interpreter of the Quebec scene he stood head and shoulders above his contemporaries, particularly in his treatment of the Canadian winter landscapes." Other critics described him as, ". . . perhaps the greatest painter of ice and snow of his generation." In France critics described him as one of the outstanding landscape painters of the North American continent. Maurice Cullen was laid to rest at Mount Royal Cemetery.

HOLLYWOOD PRODUCER: A NEWFOUNDLANDER

The first full-colour musical motion picture produced by Hollywood was *The King of Jazz*. The film, which starred Bing Crosbie, was produced and directed by a man who was born and raised on Barnes Road in St. John's. This same man helped the famous Lucille Ball get her start in Hollywood by teaching her singing and dancing, and even tutored other greats like Bob Hope, John Barrymore, Frank Sinatra and Dean Martin.

His list of students reads like a "Who's Who" of Hollywood. John Murray Anderson, who at one time was director in chief of Paramount Famous Players Theatre and also director of Radio City Music Hall, was born in St. John's on September 20, 1886.

While a young boy living in St. John's, Anderson's best friend was Ron Young. Their friendship lasted until Anderson's death in 1954. Young once told me that Anderson displayed a strong ambition to make it big in the theatrical world at a very early age. He recalled that one day the two were attending a stage production at the Nickel Theatre in St. John's. When the show was over Ron commented that his ambition in life would be to become manager of a theatre like the Nickel. Anderson replied that he wanted to create great theatrical productions. Both men fulfilled their dreams.

Ron Young did achieve his dream and became manager of the Nickel Theatre and three other theatres around St. John's. Ron's friend John Murray Anderson also achieved his dream.

In addition to tutoring the famous, Anderson created the musical and dance scenes for the Hollywood movie, *The Greatest Show on Earth*, produced and directed over thirty-five major musical comedy successes in New York and London including six editions of the *Greenwich Village Follies*.

Other productions of Anderson's included *The Music Box Revue*, *What's in a Name?*, *Dearest Enemy*, *Murray Anderson's Almanac*, and perhaps the most famous of all, *The Ziegfield Follies*.

Anderson's biggest money-maker was the *King of Jazz*. It was this film that established his reputation and made him a multimillionaire.

John Murray Anderson never forgot his childhood friend in St. John's. Whenever he returned to the city for a visit he would always look him up and on one occasion invited Ron to return to Hollywood with him and work with his firm. Ron refused the offer and opted to stay in the city he dearly loved.

Several years later Young was visited by a gentleman who told him that before leaving Hollywood John Murray Anderson had asked him to contact his friend Ron Young. The man turned out to be the world famous Robert L. Ripley. Believe it or not.

The Cantwells of Cape Spear

The 145 year reign of the Cantwell family at the Cape Spear lighthouse was made possible by Prince Henry of the Netherlands. During July 1845, Prince Henry was scheduled to visit St. John's aboard the warship *Rijyn*. When the vessel arrived in Newfoundland coastal waters there was heavy fog and the *Rijyn* went astray. Six harbour pilots were dispatched from St. John's to search for the royal man-of-war and escort it

back. Pilot Jim Cantwell located the *Rijyn* and skillfully steered the large vessel through the heavy fog and into St. John's harbour.

The Dutch prince was impressed and appreciative of Cantwell's ability. Prince Henry asked to meet Cantwell in order to personally thank him. After expressing his gratitude the prince told Cantwell to name his reward. Cantwell asked that he be given the job as lighthouse keeper at Cape Spear. The new lighthouse, three miles by sea from St. John's, was finished in 1836. While it was not the first lighthouse in Newfoundland, it was the first which incorporated into its structure the keeper's home and the beacon. The prince used his influence to secure the job for Cantwell and the agreement was sealed with a parchment signed by the prince and witnessed by Governor John Harvey. It was tradition thereafter that each royal visitor to St. John's would sign the parchment.

The document was last in the possession of Doug Muir, a Cantwell descendent in St. John's. Today the document is not legally valid and was questioned in 1968 when Frank Cantwell retired. His son Gerald, a competent and trained technician, had to apply and qualify for the job. He was successful and continued the Cantwell tradition of Cape Spear lighthouse keepers until his retirement.

MISCELLANEOUS
STORIES

NEWFOUNDLAND'S
FIRST WOMAN SETTLER

On June 8, 1542, Marguerite de Roberval became the first woman to set foot in Newfoundland. For three years thereafter she went through a living hell. Before coming to Newfoundland, Marguerite was the darling of French society; bright, witty and beautiful. When she learned that her uncle had been appointed by family friend King Francis I to the position of first Viceroy to Canada, she begged him to take her along.

Marguerite felt it would be adventurous and romantic to live in the frontiers of the New World. The uncle agreed to her request and Marguerite was accompanied by her nurse, an old Norman peasant woman named Damiene. During the voyage to the New World, she flirted and fell in love with a common soldier. The affair angered her uncle who held strong Calvinistic beliefs. It also damaged his French pride.

When Marguerite refused to break off the romance her uncle decided to teach her a lesson. He arranged for her marriage to protect the family name then set her ashore on a cold, drab, desolate island off the coast of Labrador known as Harrington Island. Marguerite's experience there provided the new name for the island and it became known as the Isle of Demons.

Following the marriage her uncle gave Marguerite some provisions, three guns and some ammunition. He ordered the old nurse to go with her. Her husband was to be put in chains, but he managed to grab some guns and ammunition and jumped into the water and swam ashore. The three struggled to survive their wild environment. Marguerite soon became pregnant but her child died shortly after it was born. Her husband went mad during the first winter and threw himself off a cliff. The following winter Damiene, the nurse, died leaving Marguerite alone to try and survive on her own.

Surprisingly, Marguerite showed great determination and courage. She built a tiny hut and hunted small game, while all the time watching the horizon for a ship. After a while she began hearing voices and turned to reading the New Testament to avoid becoming insane.

Three years passed and just when Marguerite was ready to give up a ship passed close to the island, saw the smoke from her camp fire and rescued her. She was still beautiful, wore an animal skin dress as her only form of clothing and was of sound mind when taken aboard the rescue vessel.

Having lost the desire for further adventure Marguerite de Roberval returned to France and became a school mistress.

THE OLD POLINA

The Newfoundland ballad "Old Polina" is well known to every Newfoundlander. It is sung at spring concerts, church and community socials, played on albums and danced to all over the province. We hear many of these ballads often and for so many years, and we sometimes wonder whether the stories told in them are really true. It was this sort of curiosity that caused me to carry out a little research into the authenticity of that famous ballad.

To begin with, there were two vessels that the story

could have dealt with. The first the *Polino*, but that vessel was lost at the Greenland whale fishery on July 11, 1891, a year before the story in the ballad took place.

The *Polino* according to Lloyd's Register of 1903 was a Montreal to St. John's cargo ship which carried flour, sugar and cheese in wooden drums. The *Polino* was a familiar sight during the latter part of the nineteenth century at Harvey's Wharf on the St. John's waterfront. It had been built in 1870 by W. Pile and Company of Sunderland, England.

Further study shows that the "Old Polina" story is actually an account of the adventures of a ship named the *Polynia* and the author may have used poetic license to call it the Polina. The *Polynia*, a 582 ton square-rigged steam-driven vessel was built at Dundee, Scotland in 1861. Its first commander was Captain Penney and during her first trip to the ice in 1862, got caught in an ice field and was driven out into Trinity Bay. During the fall of 1862, while moored at St. John's harbour, Governor Bannerman paid a visit to the *Polynia*. He went to see his old friend the ship's commander, Captain Granville. Bannerman and Granville had become friends when they met on an arctic trip several years earlier. The following year the *Polynia* went sealing and whaling in Newfoundland and Arctic waters.

During the fall of 1892 the ship was under the command of the man made famous in the ballad, Captain Guy—"and Captain Guy that daring boy, came plunging through the sea." The *Polynia* was on a trip from Dundee to St. John's. Just two days after leaving port the it struck a heavy southwest gale that killed one of the crew and injured ten others. The heavy gale carried away the lifeboats and damaged her structure.

Guy noted in his logbook that it appeared to be a tidal wave as it came and disappeared quickly. The ballad refers to this:

> It washed away our quarter deck
> Our stanchion just as well,
> and so we left the whole shebang,
> afloating in the gale.

After weathering the storm in the fall of that year, which supplied the material for the ballad, the *Polynia* went to the seal fishery with Guy in command and brought back almost twenty thousand pelts. It took part in the famous arctic search for Sir John Franklin and was the first full-rigged steam engine to enter St. John's. On July 11, 1892, Guy and his crew of thirty-seven abandoned ship after she became caught in the ice. The next day she went to the bottom. Guy later retired to live the remainder of his life at Dundee, Scotland.

Some History of Her Majesty's Penitentiary

From the time Her Majesty's Penitentiary on Forest Road went into operation on August 24, 1859, until the date of the last hanging on May 22, 1942, five people went to the gallows inside its walls. The five were: Patrick Geehan, 1872; William Parnell, 1889; Francis Canning, 1899; Wo Fen Game, 1922; and Herbert Spratt, 1942.

Prior to opening the penitentiary, hangings took place from the old courthouse just off Duckworth Street. Constructed in 1730 this wooden building combined a prison with a courthouse. Conditions were intolerable. As many as ten men would often share the same cell and each person was required to pay fifteen cents per day for his keep. Because of these poor conditions, in 1825, Governor Cochrane requested and received permission to construct a prison of stone and once more the new building combined the courthouse with the prison.

The interior of the new prison was as distressing as the old one. There was a long corridor of cells with the hallway dimly lit by lanterns. A limited amount of fresh air circulated into the cells from a small window built into each cell door. The only light in the cells was the light that crept into the cracks in the door or the small windows.

On June 9, 1846, a great fire swept St. John's and this structure was completely destroyed. Faced with the problem of housing prisoners, authorities set up facilities at an abandoned army barracks on Signal Hill. This building became the first separate prison in St. John's. Prisoners were housed in the middle of three adjoining buildings. The other two had their roofs blown off in a heavy wind storm. The prison was considered to be a dangerous place during heavy winds and the jailers had to be prepared to evacuate the premises at a moment's notice.

An attempt to construct a prison was made at the site of the present penitentiary in 1852, and a basement was partly constructed. However, due to financial cutbacks by the government of the day, construction on the project was stopped. On orders from the government the thirty thousand Irish bricks which were to be used for the prison construction were auctioned off. The auction took place on August 5, 1856, and the highest bidder was Bishop John Mullock who purchased the stone for use in building St. Bon's College.

The need for a prison became a priority as the Signal Hill prison deteriorated, and in 1858 the present penitentiary was constructed. Prisoners were transferred from Signal Hill to the new building on August 24, 1859, and Richard Brace became the first person to run the prison.

𝒫RISONERS ℳUST 𝒫AY

During the early nineteenth century the Newfoundland government allowed only sixpence a day to look after prisoners in St. John's. This amount was not enough to provide even a basic subsistence for the imprisoned, and the jail keeper, Richard Perchard, who petitioned the magistrates for an increase in prisoner's allowance.

The petition read:

> The petition of Richard Perchard most humbly sheweth that your petitioner is keeper of His Majesty's gaol of this place (St. John's) and that he has served in that capacity about two years. That during that period it has been his misfortune to have had charge of a great number of prisoners, many of them convicted felons, of which latter he has occasionally had to the number of eight at a time.
>
> That for the support of such persons your petitioner is only allowed by the district the small stipend of sixpence each per day. That such prisoners being composed chiefly

of labouring men, your petitioner finds six-pence a day very insufficient for their main-tenance and that the bread and water with which they are supplied often cost him more than the amount of such allowance, com-mon humanity forbidding him to increase their necessary sufferings by the cravings of hunger, but that such demands are in a cer-tain degree an injury to the petitioner's own numerous family.

That your petitioner is nevertheless very grateful for his appointment to the said office, but is persuaded that when the pres-ent rate of allowance was fixed it was deemed adequate to cover all necessary expenses, which he finds it not to be.

In conclusion the petition stated:

Your petitioner therefore humbly prays that your worships will be pleased to take into consideration and endeavour to procure for him such additional allowances for the maintenance of prisoners in the said gaol as your worships may think reasonable ... and as in duty bound will ever pay ... signed
Richard Perchard.

The chief magistrate for Newfoundland turned the petition over to Governor C. Hamilton and on October 20, 1823, a reply was received, addressed to the magistrate from Hamilton. Governor Hamilton sympathized with the plight of Perchard, but said the government could not afford to increase the allowances, yet he did offer the jailer a solution. Hamilton gave Perchard the authority to charge the prisoners for their keep while in prison. The governor advised that in the future Perchard should charge each prisoner nine pence per day for board and lodging.

Two years later the grand jury inspected the jail and determined it had deteriorated into a very bad state of repair and was no longer suitable for the purpose for which it was intended.

Aviation History

June 14 marks one of the most important anniversaries in world aviation history. On this day in 1919 the first nonstop Atlantic flight was made by the duo of Captain John Alcock and Lieutenant Arthur Brown. The famous pilots flew their *Vickers-Vimey* aircraft from Lester's Field in St. John's to Clifden, Ireland, in less than sixteen hours.

Although Alcock and Brown were the first to make the non-stop Atlantic crossing, their limelight was stolen for almost thirty years by Charles Lindbergh who made the first solo non-stop Atlantic crossing a few years after Alcock and Brown's daring achievement.

This may be attributed to the American tendency — and their great ability — to promote and glorify their own heroes. The achievement of Alcock and Brown was overshadowed by the adulation given Lindbergh and they were forgotten for almost thirty years.

It took great courage, planning and skill to overcome the many obstacles of a transatlantic flight. When the British duo set out from St. John's they carried 870 gallons of gas and forty gallons of oil. From the time of takeoff at 1:58 p.m. on Saturday, June 14,

1919, the *Vickers-Vimey* experienced trouble. On take-off, because the aircraft was overloaded, they had trouble clearing Signal Hill. Then their wireless radio failed due to a broken generator. They were able to receive messages but were unable to transmit any. Three hundred miles out of St. John's, flames burst from the exhaust and the pilots were unable to put the fire out, but fortunately the exhaust fell into the Atlantic Ocean. In spite of the difficulties the two continued on with their attempt to fly across the Atlantic. When darkness descended they were plagued with even more trouble. Heavy clouds obscured the moon and the duo kept the plane as close to the water as possible. The temperature dropped causing the wings to ice up. At times Alcock and Brown had no idea as to which direction they were flying. On one occasion the heavy ice caused the craft to nosedive towards the ocean almost one hundred feet before they managed to pull her up. As dawn approached their luck changed. Temperatures rose and the ice began melting. The aircraft became easier to handle. At 8:30 a.m. on June 15, residents of Clifden, Ireland, heard the sound of engines overhead. The *Vickers-Vimey* came into view, rolled erratically and set down in a field, nose-diving into the mud. Alcock and Brown had become the first to fly nonstop across the Atlantic. They won their £10,000 prize (equivalent to $50,000 at the exchange rate of the day) put up by the London *Daily Mail* for their accomplishment. The prize was presented to them by Sir Winston Churchill at the Savoy Hotel in London. They were both knighted by King George V in recognition of their feat.

On December 19, 1919, Alcock was killed in a plane crash in France. Brown never flew again after Alcock's death. He passed away in 1948. A replica of the *Vickers-Vimey* flown by the two pilots was donated to City Hall on December 2, 1973, by McLoughlan Supplies Limited of St. John's.

THE BREMEN

On the morning of April 12, 1928, the aircraft *Bremen* departed from Baldonnel airfield in Ireland in an attempt to make the first east to west nonstop transatlantic flight. The *Bremen* was flown by the Irishman, Major James Fitzmaurice of the Irish Free State Army, and two Germans, Captain Herman Koehl and Baron Van Huenfeld.

The aircraft was owned by Van Huenfeld who paid for it and was underwriting the cost of the attempted Atlantic crossing. The flight marked the fourth effort to fly east-west across the Atlantic following the successful west-east crossing made by Alcock and Brown. World attention was focused on the flight and news media from all over the world were monitoring the event.

While the trio prepared for takeoff they gathered weather reports from Nova Scotia, Washington and Boston. The reports were not favourable. A storm was predicted over Nova Scotia; Washington forecast high winds; heavy rain was expected in the Boston region; and the en route forecast indicated head winds for most of the journey. As in the Alcock and Brown case, the competition to establish an aviation record was keen. Two other flying teams were preparing to make the same flying attempt. They were the team of Hinchclifte and McKay and the French flyers Detroyat, Poillard and Droiuhim.

The pressure of this competition influenced Van

Huenfeld to take the gamble. For eighteen hours after takeoff the aviators fought heavy wind, rain, snow and fog. After thirty-six hours flying time, they sighted a lighthouse. Flying at sixteen hundred feet they searched the area for a suitable landing site. The only level stretch they could find was an icefield. Captain Koehl took control of the plane and brought her down on the treacherous ice runway. Upon contact with the ice the *Bremen* rolled over but was suddenly pulled up by an ice ridge. This historic flight had made a connection with Newfoundland. The *Bremen* had landed at Greenbay Island which measures a mile long and a mile wide and is located a mile off the coast of Labrador in the Straits of Belle Isle.

The first to greet the aviation heroes were the lighthouse keeper's wife, Madame Le Templier and three Newfoundlanders, Albert Rose, Arthur Rose and Charles Spurrell. Word of the landing was relayed to Boston and a rescue team headed by Bernt Balchen and Floyd Bennett was sent to the scene. Balchen flew the *Bremen* to New York. During that flight Bennett developed pneumonia and later died. Reports of the *Bremen*'s success were flashed all over the world and the city of New York gave the three heroes one of its best ticker tape parades.

REID THE AVIATOR

Leonard Reid, son of Sir Robert Reid of the Reid Newfoundland Company, made Canadian aviation history on August 8, 1934, when he and James Ayling became the first Canadians to successfully fly from Canada to Europe. With the exception of Errol Boyd, they were the only two Canadians to make the successful Atlantic crossing up until World War Two. Initially the two set out from Wasaga intending to fly to Baghdad but technical problems and bad weather forced them to cut the trip short and land at London.

The plane flown on this historic occasion was a de Havilland Dragon which was owned by Jim and Amy Mollison but never used. Reid christened the plane *The Trail of the Caribou*. Noted Canadian aviation historian Frank Ellis referred to the takeoff stating, "The getaway was a touch and go affair with disaster hanging in the balance as the heavily loaded ship sped down the long beach. The airmen covered nine miles in the cross-wind before the plane rose saggily into the air."

As the *Caribou* ascended higher and higher into the air, ice caused the throttle to stick at wide open. In an effort to free the throttle the control was slightly bent. The flyers were unable to reach it in the air and decided not to tamper with it because they feared jamming it for good. The wide open throttle caused high fuel consumption and it became necessary to put down at London. When they landed they had only two hundred gallons of gas left.

Reid and Ayling established the record as being the first pilots to fly an airplane from Canada to England. A monument in recognition of their splendid achievement stands at Wasaga Beach, Ontario.

LADY PEACE

During September 1936 two pilots, employed by World War I ace Eddie Rickenbacker, were attempting to set a flight record from New York to England and back when their plane developed trouble and crashed into bog near Musgrave Harbour. The plane they were flying was the famous *Lady Peace* and the progress of the record setting attempt was being monitored by news agencies all over the world. The two pilots were Harry Richman and Dick Merrill. At 2:00 p.m. on September 13, 1936, the radio operator at Carmanville spotted a silver coloured plane circling very low and in less than fifteen minutes it disappeared. The monoplane had succeeded in making it to England and was on its return flight to New York. It had taken the *Lady Peace* fourteen and a half hours to reach Newfoundland. As she approached the Musgrave Harbour area she ran out of fuel and crash-landed in the bog. News of the accident was flashed by radio and newspapers all over the world and many prominent U.S. and Canadian journalists came to Newfoundland to cover the story.

Several hours after the crash the two airmen were rescued and taken to the home of T. W. Abbott. Rickenbacker himself flew up from New York with a mechanic and fuel to get the plane flying again. Rickenbacker described the crossing of the *Lady Peace* as a remarkable achievement.

As in the Banting tragedy, the good people of Musgrave Harbour came to the aid of the Americans. They towed the *Lady Peace* from the bog and constructed a wooden runway on the beach which enabled the American pilots to get their historic plane back into the air. The *Lady Peace* was the first aircraft to make a return trip to Europe from North America.

Commenting on the greatly publicized event one newspaper editorialized, "They sighted no savage beasts. They encountered no primitive savages. The

140

Lady Peace might have dug her nose into far worse places than a Newfoundland bog."

THE HOAX OF
THE CENTURY

This incident actually happened and it had all Europe and the United States rocking with laughter. Some describe it as the hoax of the century and it may well be. The episode took place in 1933 at Paris, France. At that time the French Chamber of Deputies had spent weeks discussing debts owed to the U.S. by European countries as a result of "The Great War." All public attention was focused on the war debts and for weeks it was the topic of conversation no matter where you went.

Every member of the Chamber was putting his two cents worth into the discussion. Three university students attentively following the legislative session were convinced that some of the deputies knew nothing about the United States or the western hemisphere. So the trio decided to do something about it. They set out to prove the ignorance of the French politicians. A few days later seventy-two members of the Chamber of Deputies received a professionally typewritten letter. The letterhead was printed, "Paris Branch, Ethnical Defence League of Newfoundlanders and Guatemalans, New York Headquarters, 43 Seventy-Second Street, New York."

The letter began with an appeal to President Roosevelt and then went on to say, "You know that two states of the Republic of the United States are deprived of a majority of the privileges enjoyed by the other forty-two. They are the states of Newfoundland and Guatemala. Newfoundland as you know is inhabited by two million people of Spanish origin who still speak Spanish since Cortés conquered the country for the Incas; while the Guatemalans speak Portuguese.

"As just one example of injustice; these two states are represented in the United States Senate by only one senator, whereas others such as New York have twelve senators." The letter continued along this vein mixing facts with fiction and when the media picked up the story all France laughed along with Americans as they learned of the league.

The funniest part of the hoax was that out of the seventy-two deputies to whom the letter was sent, nine wrote back to the Ethnical Defence League of Newfoundlanders and Guatemalans promising undying support.

THE
NEWFOUNDLAND FLAG

The pink the rose of England shows,
The green St. Patrick's emblem bright
While in between, the spotless sheen
Of Andrew's Cross displays the white

These are the first lines of the Newfoundland patriotic song entitled, "The Flag of Newfoundland," and describe the Newfoundland's original flag, the famous Pink, White and Green. The same Newfoundland flag that Captain Bob Bartlett planted six miles from the North Pole on July 4, 1908. Bartlett was the first white man to reach so far north and he remained at this point to allow Admiral Perry to make his final dash to the Pole.

A valiant effort was made during the 1970s to persuade the provincial government to adopt this flag as the provincial flag of Newfoundland. The Newfoundland Historical Society, the St. John's Folk Arts Council and the Newfoundland Historic Trust presented a well-researched and documented brief supporting the Pink, White and Green but their case had little effect on legislative members who decided on adopting a new distinctive flag instead of the old Pink, White and Green. Although the old flag is out, its story is worth preserving.

During the nineteenth century there was a great deal of friction between new immigrants to the country and the long established settlers. The friction grew into open conflict when it appeared that the new Newfoundlanders were getting their pick of political patronage jobs and favours over the natives or bushborns as they were known. To advance and protect their interests, the bushborns organized the Native Society and adopted a native flag. This new flag had a green spruce tree on a pink background, and under the tree were two clasped hands and the motto Philanthropy.

In those days men came to St. John's annually from all over Newfoundland to seek work on the large fleet of sealing vessels operating from this port. In 1844 over six thousand such men converged on the city. The presence of these men was of major concern to authorities because of the constant bickering between the bushborn natives and the new Newfoundlanders. To deal with the problem, authorities came up with a program to put the men to work while waiting for their ships to leave. The program was the famous "wood haul" whereby the men would cut and haul firewood from surrounding forests for use by local churches, schools and other institutions.

As each group completed a woodpile they would decorate it with bunting and flags. The natives flew their pink flag, the immigrants a green banner. In February 1843 an argument between the groups over which had the largest wood haul erupted into a brawl with many people being injured. When Bishop Fleming heard of it he brought the ringleaders together, gave them a long lecture and recommended that they join the Pink and Green together in a show of new unity and understanding. This was done by inserting a piece of neutral white in between; and the Pink, White and Green flag of Newfoundland was born.